A Cook's Journey

SLOW FOOD IN THE HEARTLAND

KURT MICHAEL FRIESE

ICE CUBE PRESS
NORTH LIBERTY, IOWA

A Cook's Journey: Slow Food In The Heartland

Copyright © 2008 Kurt Michael Friese

ISBN 9781888160369

Library of Congress Control Number: 2008923646

Ice Cube Press (est. 1993)
205 North Front Street
North Liberty, Iowa 52317-9302
www.icecubepress.com
steve@icecubepress.com

Manufactured in the United States of America. Part of the Green Paper Initiative with Thomson-Shore Printing, Dexter, Michigan. See the Eco-audit below.

The paper used in this publication meets the minimum requirements of the American National Standard for Information Sciences—Permanence of Paper for Printed Library Materials, ANSI Z39.48-1992

All photographs © Kurt Michael Friese except author photo © by Danny Wilcox Frazier/Redux

Ice Cube Press is committed to preserving ancient forests and natural resources. We elected to print this title on 30% post consumer recycled paper, processed chlorine free. As a result, for this printing, we have saved:

2 Trees (40' tall and 6-8" diameter)
893 Gallons of Wastewater
2 million BTU's of Total Energy
115 Pounds of Solid Waste
215 Pounds of Greenhouse Gases

Ice Cube Press made this paper choice because our printer, Thomson-Shore, Inc., is a member of Green Press Initiative, a nonprofit program dedicated to supporting authors, publishers, and suppliers in their efforts to reduce their use of fiber obtained from endangered forests.

 For more information, visit www.greenpressinitiative.org

Environmental impact estimates were made using the Environmental Defense Paper Calculator. For more information visit: www.papercalculator.org.

To Kim, Devon, and Taylor,
my true sources of sustenance and joy

"Saying you have no time to cook is like saying you have no time to bathe."
-Marcella Hazan

CONTENTS

Community & Outreach

Appendices

Acknowledgements

The list of people who have helped to make this book possible has grown impossibly long. No longer will I poke fun at the Academy Award winners who stumble over trying to get all their thank-yous out in a prescribed time.

First a big thanks to thank Steve Semken and Ice Cube Press, who liberated this book to make it what it was meant to be.

All the subjects of this book deserve great thanks of course. They displayed tremendous tolerance of me invading their lives, then forcing them to read and fact-check the essays. Here it is, y'all, I hope you like it. My deepest gratitude to the farmers, artisans, chefs, Slow Food members and so many others who are included in this book. Meeting each of you has enriched my life, and you were very kind to spend time with me.

Many thanks to the members, convivium leaders (and former leaders!) of Slow Food throughout the Heartland who helped me track down these wonderful stories, and often fed and sheltered me along the way:

Debbie Apple, Christine Barbour, Susan Boldt, Rebecca Bryant, Arlene Coco Buscombe, Conrad Cortellini, Deborah Deacon, Bernadette Dryden, Amanda Edmonds, Ava Fajen, Martha Folk, Kamala Gamble, Kelly Gibson, Lisa Guillory, Neil Hamilton, Ronald Huff, Mike Hursey, Jack Kaestner, Paul Landeck, Tami Lax, Janine MacLachlan, Rebecca Marsh, Lawrence Mate, Jasper Mirabile, Kerry Norman, Treva Reimer, David Robb, Jesse Salzwedel, Jo Ann Simpson, Grace Singleton, Joel Smith, and David Tallent. You are all wonderful hosts and guides.

The folks at Slow Food's National Office in New York, first under Patrick Martins' able guidance and since 2004 with Ericka Lesser at the helm, are always there to help any Slow Food member. Staff past and present, Yuri Asano, Julia DeMartini-Day, Makalé Faber-Cullen, Gina Fiorello-Brady, Sara Firebaugh, Deena Goldman, Jerusha Klemperer, Cerise Mayo, Ragan Rhyne, Kakee Scott, Jenny Trotter, Cecily Upton, Winnie Yang and Sarah Weiner, you have remarkable patience with a demanding old man, thank you.

Terry and Peggy Loveless, thanks for always having a cold beer handy when I needed one.

Speaking of patience, a tremendous thank you to my mother and father, Patricia and George Friese, who taught me the importance of an education and despite all the roadblocks I threw in my own way still made all things possible. David Taylor, you taught me to keep my chin up and soldier on against difficult odds, thanks for that. Many thanks to my sister Chrissy, who has been a wonderful tutor and project manager, and who put the "Recommended Reading" section in the correct format.

I owe the survival of my restaurant to the best dang crew in town. Jered Dieter, Kevin Henning, Dan Knowles, Jeremy Tole and Patrick Weeg in the kitchen and Jill Kinkade, Kate Papenthien, Constie Brown, Alyssa Bonkosi-Cress, Corbin Booth and Morgan Weiss in the dining room, as well as the many others who came before and since. You guys are the best. And my thanks to Tony Christner, who keeps the books in line.

Thanks also to the members of Slow Food Iowa, who have been tolerant of my spotty record as convivium director while I've been researching the book. And, if you are the inevitable person who I should have remembered to list here and I didn't, please know that I am as grateful as I am absent-minded

Most of all my eternal love and gratitude to Kim, Devon, and Taylor - my wife, son, and daughter - to whom this book is dedicated. You are my inspiration and, like everything I do, this book is for you.

Introduction

My whole life has always revolved around food. From the times my mother had me stand on a stool in our Columbus, Ohio, kitchen and stir the raisin sauce for the Easter ham, to the lunches where all my family talked about was what to have for dinner, to summer jobs, college, and a career in the industry, life has always been about food. If I display any passion for food, it comes from a lifetime of appreciating it, studying it, and sometimes literally wallowing in it.

I have been working in the food business since 1979, honing skills and developing tastes that have led me to understand the truest fact of the culinary arts: fresh tastes best.

Inspired by the work of Alice Waters at Chez Panisse in Berkeley, when I finished college I realized that I wanted a career in food, and so attended the New England Culinary Institute near Burlington, Vermont, where I later taught. I helped build a garden there, and finally saw first hand the difference between food that came off a truck and food that came in the kitchen door from the garden. Also, the rewards of meeting the Vermont growers who produced such magnificent ingredients had a profound effect on me. It became very important to shake the hand that raised the food.

When I returned to the Heartland in 1992 I was amazed at the dichotomy I found here. It appeared to me that the richest soil on the planet was being used primarily to grow not food, but feed. Farmers' markets, with the notable exception of the Dane County market in Madison, Wisconsin, were rare and inconsistently controlled. Most restaurants outside the major metropolitan areas (and even in some of them) were the same repetitious, assembly-line corporate chains in every town, making each place seem just like the last one.

Since that time, a quiet revolution has occurred, as people all over the Heartland, and all over America and the world, reawaken to the beauty, importance and flavor of fresh, homemade, real food. Where once a restaurant might be judged by the distant and exotic sources of its ingredients, today the best restaurants are known for getting their food from just down the road. The names of farms and farmers are sprinkled throughout menus as if they themselves were vital ingredients, because they are. Today Iowa has more farmer's markets per capita than any state in the Union.

The best way to insure the freshness of a product is to get it straight from the farmer who raised it, or the artisan who crafted it. When I shake the hand that raised the food, I know the farmer cares about the food and the land. When I can still feel the field heat radiating from the tomato as I slice into it on a hot August afternoon, then I know I have something truly special to share with my guests.

For some time I lived under the mistaken illusion that there were only a handful of us in the world, even fewer in the Heartland, who professed these ideas that seemed so self-evident. It was in 1999 that I discovered that there were tens of thousands of people around the world who felt as I did. They were already well organized, and had even given a name to their movement to counteract the deleterious effects of fast food and the standardization of flavors. They called it Slow Food. As sometimes happens to those in my profession, my ego had gotten the better of me. I thought I was on the cutting edge, but instead I was way behind.

What is Slow Food? To understand it fully, one must at first separate the movement from the food for a moment, even though they are actually inexorably linked. The movement, the worldwide organization, exists to connect food and pleasure with responsibility and awareness. It does so through a wide array of activities, events and publications ranging from the very small and local to the very large and global. To know if the dish you are preparing is Slow Food, do not consider how long it takes to make, but simply consider this: If the food is raised with care, prepared with passion, and served with love, then it is "Slow" food no matter who makes it.

Many people have said to me, after listening to me proselytize about Slow Food for a while, "sure that sounds great, but how am I supposed to actually do that with my crazy schedule?" There are many examples in this book, but the first is slow down. Take a breath. Stop and smell the bacon. Take stock of what is truly important in your life, and cull a few of the things that don't make the list. Slow Food founder and President Carlo Petrini said it best, "We are all going to the same place. Let us go there slowly."

The movement began in the mid-1980s as a fairly straightforward gourmet society in Italy called Arcigola. When members learned to their horror that McDonald's, the antithesis of all they held dear, was coming to Italy, they were indignant. Not only was this bastion of industrialized food coming to the culinary epicenter of the western world, but also McDonald's had the temerity to put a store at the foot of the Spanish Steps, on the Piazza de Spagna in Rome. This was seen by the members of Arcigola as akin to opening a pork butchery in Jerusalem.

Arcigola organized a protest, feeding homemade Penne Pomadoro to thousands on the Piazza on McDonald's opening day. Though the rally was a great success, they realized then that this could not merely be one last scream into the abyss followed by complacent resignation. They decided to mount "a firm defense of quiet material pleasure." In 1989, an international meeting of like-minded members met in Paris. Throughout Europe, the English term "fast food" was used by everyone to describe the sort of food they opposed, so they chose the English language for the new name of the organization – Slow Food.

They wrote and ratified what they called *The Slow Food Manifesto*, which inspires its readers to "rediscover the flavors and savors of regional cooking," and challenges them to create an "international exchange of experiences, knowledge, projects."

This statement was their line in the soil. No longer would they be idle gourmets, content to stand aside as their cherished food traditions were swept aside by the forces of standardization.

Somewhat contrary to its name, Slow Food spread its ecogastronomic message rapidly across the globe. By 2006 it had nearly 100,000 members in over 100 countries, 15,000 of which are in the United States of America – only Italy itself has more. Its flagship biennial event, the Salone del Gusto ("hall of flavor"), is the largest event of its kind in the world, hosting more than 150,000 visitors over five days.

In 2004, three massive undertakings were successfully launched: The Slow Food Foundation for Biodiversity, which aims to protect endangered food species; and The University of Gastronomic Sciences, the first of its kind in the world, opened their doors. Perhaps Slow Food's most innovative accomplishment, however, was Terra Madre: A World Gathering of Food Communities, which comprised a meeting of 5000 sustainable farmers and traditional food artisans from 120 countries in an effort to create a global network for the sustainable food world to rival that of the agro-industrial complex. More than 500 of the delegates were from the United States, 92 of them were from the Heartland, and a handful of them are discussed in this book. Terra Madre was so successful that they repeated it in 2006, and added 500 educators and 1000 chefs, myself included.

For the purposes of this book, "the Heartland" is defined as a thirteen state region that stretches from Ohio to Oklahoma to North Dakota. Over a period of four years, guided by friends and Slow Food members throughout the Heartland, I sought out stories of people who were living the ideals of a slower way of life, whether they were members of the formal movement or not. I found plenty of stories in my travels, too many to include them all, but I've chosen 34 of them and divided them into our categories: Farmers, Artisans, Restaurants and Markets, and Community and Outreach. Each is intended to show a different aspect of food and the slow life, from the farms where it starts, through the skilled beautiful places where the food is prepared, to the people who are helping to spread the word.

While this is not an "official" Slow Food publication, you will read stories of people who epitomize the ideals of "slow" living on an everyday basis, and find recipes that are either by them or are inspired by them. Some are dues-paying members of Slow Food USA; some are not. What matters is that they have all come to realize the futility of today's fast-paced fast food world. Here are stories of people who have learned that old-fashioned does not mean outdated, that quality does trump quantity, and that there are serious, hidden costs to "cheap" food.

They all understand something more as well, and you will probably agree. If you look back at the best moments of your life, the top-ten, all-time happiest times, you are likely to find that many, perhaps most were spent at a table, with great food in front of you and people you love around you. That is what the movement is all about. The people in this book are living the ideals set forth in the Slow Food USA mission statement:

> Slow Food USA envisions a future food system that is based on the principles of high quality and taste, environmental sustainability, and social justice—in essence, a food system that is good, clean and fair. We seek to catalyze a broad cultural shift away from the destructive effects of an industrial food system and fast life; toward the regenerative cultural, social and economic benefits of a sustainable food system, regional food traditions, the pleasures of the table, and a slower and more harmonious rhythm of life.

As of this writing, in nearly 35 convivia throughout the Heartland, thousands of people who care about their families and their health, their palates and their planet are joining the movement to help save the world's best things. Of course there are plenty of ways to live slowly without being a formal member of a movement. Plant a garden, shop at a farmers' market, visit a farm.

People all over the Heartland, and all over the world are discovering the joy of slow living. In these pages you will find just a handful of their stories.

A Note About the Recipes

I did not set out to write a cookbook, and this is not one. The recipes are meant to illustrate the delicious possibilities that occur when fresh food is prepared and served communally, and when the farmers support the community who in turn support the farmers.

Most of the recipes in this book are the creations of the people discussed here. This is not fancy food, and you should dispel any notion that Slow Food and "fancy food" are synonymous. Always remember the simple rule I mention throughout the book: If it is raised with care, prepared with passion and served with love, then it is Slow Food.

I have tweaked the recipes here and there, trying to make them simple to follow while maintaining the integrity of the original recipe.

A few of the recipes are my own, which are often served at my Iowa City restaurant, Devotay.

As with any recipe, always read through the entire recipe start to finish before you even touch any food or kitchen tools. Make sure you understand the procedures before you begin. Then build what professionals call your *Mise en Place*, a French term that translates to "everything in place". Pre-measure all ingredients, locate all tools (knives, pans, wooden spoons, whatever) and have them at the ready. You will find cooking to be much simpler and more enjoyable if you are not, for example, frantically trying to open a bottle of wine as the meat you are sautéing is passing the optimum deglazing point.

You will find an array of dishes here, and by using them as a guide you can begin to create a meal of heirloom pumpkin soup from Simone Delaty of Simone's Plain and Simple in Wellman, Iowa alongside "beer-can" chicken from Julie and Tim Walker of Greystone Farm in Fayette, Missouri. Then you could accompany your Thanksgiving "heritage" turkey with wild rice dressing made with Manoomin from Winona LaDuke at the White Earth Land Recovery Project in Ponsford, Minnesota, and an apple-pecan stuffing from my own restaurant using heirloom apples from your local orchard.

Use the recipes, and the rest of the book, as inspiration to helping you living a slower way of life.

Recipes

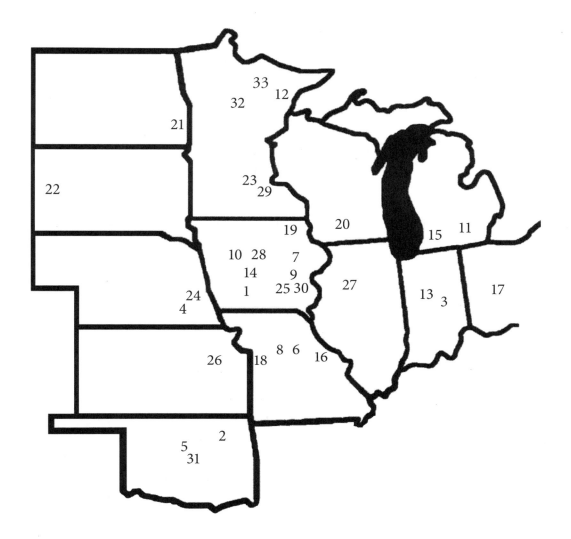

1. Winterset Iowa
2. Claremore, Oklahoma
3. McCordsville, Indiana
4. Raymond, Nebraska
5. Guthrie, Oklahoma
6. Harrisburg, Missouri
7. Strawberry Point, Iowa
8. Fayette, Missouri
9. Solon, Iowa
10. Templeton, Iowa
11. Ann Arbor, Michigan
12. Knife River, Minnesota
13. Zionsville, Indiana
14. Norwalk, Iowa
15. Buchanan, Michigan
16. St Louis, Missouri
17. Columbus, Ohio
18. Kansas City, Missouri
19. Decorah, Iowa
20. Madison, Wisconsin
21. Fargo, North Dakota
22. Rapid City, South Dakota
23. Minneapolis, Minnesota
24. Lincoln, Nebraska
25. Iowa City, Iowa
26. Lawrence, Kansas
27. Congerville, Illinois
28. Ames, Iowa
29. St. Paul, Minnesota
30. West Branch, Iowa
31. Oklahoma City, Oklahoma
32. Ponsford, Minnesota
33. Chisholm, Minnesota

FARMERS

"In the long view, no nation is healthier than its children, or more prosperous than its farmers."
—President Harry S Truman, at the signing of the School Lunch Act, 1946

"Chemical fertilizers and pesticides are necessary only as a crutch for the weaknesses of industrial food production."
—Elliot Coleman, Four-Season Harvest

An Apple by Any Other Name

Winterset, Iowa, and the Birth of Delicious.

MADISON COUNTY, IA - One cool spring morning, about 1880, Madison County farmer Jesse Hiatt was walking the rows of his young orchard when he noticed a chance seedling growing between the rows. Being an orderly man, he preferred that his trees grow in an organized fashion, and he chopped the seedling down. The seedling grew back the following year, and so he chopped it down again. When the seedling sprouted back up a third time, legend has it Mr. Hiatt said to the tree, "If thee must grow, thee may."

Hiatt nurtured the tree for ten years. When it finally came to fruition, Hiatt was pleased with the red and yellow streaked appearance and the sweet, impressive flavor. He named it the Hawkeye after his adopted home state and began to seek a nursery to propagate his discovery. Eight or ten of them turned him down before his big break came.

He sent some of the fruit to a contest in Louisiana, Missouri, which was seeking new varieties of fruit trees, especially apples. The Stark Brothers Fruit Company held the competition as part of their search for an apple tree to replace the then most popular tree, the Ben Davis. The Ben Davis had a nice appearance and was durable in shipping, was weather hardy, but lacked flavor. When Clarence Stark tasted the apple with the unusual oblong shape and the distinctive five bumps on the bottom, he pronounced it "Delicious!" Unfortunately, due to some poor record keeping, Hiatt's name and address were lost and it wasn't until Hiatt re-entered the competition the following year that his Hawkeye was officially declared the winner.

The Stark Brothers Fruit Company bought the rights to Hiatt's discovery and began taking cuttings from the original tree at Hiatt's Winterset farm. Study led them to the conclusion that this new variety was probably the result of an accidental cross of two very old varieties, the Bellflower and the Winesap. Sixty years later, Stark had sold more than 10,000,000 trees world wide that were all descendants of that original tree. They had renamed Hiatt's Hawkeye after Clarence Stark's original pronouncement, and the Delicious apple was on its way to becoming the most popular apple variety in the world.

Back in Winterset, the original tree continued to flourish in a state that was second only to Michigan in apple production. In 1940, on Armistice Day, a ferocious ice storm leveled Iowa's orchards, a blast from which Iowa's apple industry would never fully recover. With orchards being expensive to replant and war on the horizon, most orchards were turned into corn and soybean fields. Hiatt's Hawkeye was split in two during the storm, and newspapers and radio commentators across the state lamented the demise of the historic tree. As Hiatt had noted all those years ago, though, this little tree "must grow." The following spring it sent up a new sprout, Phoenix-like, right from the middle of the split and it thrives to this day not far from the historic covered bridges in Madison County. It has a monument to it, a fence and a private horticulturist to protect it, as well as a festival in its honor in Donnellson, Iowa.

Today, the fruit that bears the Delicious name bears little resemblance to that original Hawkeye. The yellow streaks are gone, replaced by a bright red shine. They are bred for shelf life, durability, and crunch, but have lost their original flavor. Ironic that it now resembles the very same attributes of the Ben Davis that led Stark to seek a replacement.

Through the efforts of the Leopold Center for Sustainable Agriculture at Iowa State University and the Seed Saver's Exchange in Decorah, Iowa, cuttings from the original tree have been propagated. At Wilson's Orchard in Iowa City, owner "Chug" Wilson's Hawkeye trees have been bearing fruit since 2002, and visitors can pick those apples along with many dozens of other varieties at Wilson's every fall. One can even enjoy a piping hot apple turnover while strolling through the scenic orchard, or enjoy a guided tour on a wagon, towed by Chug himself in his big-brimmed hat.

Strolling amidst the well-tended rows of apples, you can feel almost instantly at peace. There is no traffic noise, no blaring advertisements, no background static; only the occasional tickling buzz of a honey bee flying by to see who is appreciating his work. In mid to late October, the trees are usually heavy-laden with yellow, blush, red and gold. Chug Wilson called the 2006 crop "a limb-buster," which was a welcome relief after 2005's disastrous late spring freeze, which wiped out the blooms on Wilson's trees and left them with a harvest of zero. In 2007, the blossoms froze again.

"We had to import apples from Wisconsin" to sell in the orchard store, Chug told me during that visit. "Never had to do that before."

Like all farming, growing apples is a very challenging undertaking, subject to the whims of weather, the market, insects, environment and urban sprawl. Joyce and Chug Wilson know these challenges all too well and have had plenty of offers from land developers to plow their trees under in favor of zero-lots or split-level ranches. They've been tempted, but have never relinquished the land. It's far too valuable to them as it is, which you can see when you catch the glint in Chug's eye when he so much as talks about his apples, or when you see Joyce pull her magnificent apple turnovers from the oven in the orchard store.

The idea behind their effort to preserve and revitalize the original Hawkeye apple is not only to acknowledge the important contribution that it made to the apple industry, but also to insure that a particular flavor – one of 140 varieties on Wilson's 80 acres – is not lost forever.

Apple-Pecan Stuffing

The original Hawkeye apple held up to cooking better than its modern-day descendant, but if you cannot get Hawkeyes in your area, many other heirloom apples work well. Visit your local orchard.

This stuffing is delicious on its own, or can be stuffed into a pork chop topped with caramelized onions for a great seasonal entrée.

    ¼ cup butter
    2 cups Hawkeye or Granny Smith Apples (about 4 apples)
    ¾ cup pecans, dry-roasted
    1 yellow onion, diced
    1 stalk celery, diced
    2 tablespoons fresh sage
    1 tablespoon salt
    1 tablespoon cracked black pepper
    1 loaf French bread, diced
    1 quart homemade chicken stock

Melt the butter in a large sauté pan over medium high heat. Sauté the apples, pecans, onion, and celery in the sauté pan until just tender. Add the sage, salt and pepper. Add the bread and mix thoroughly. Add the stock, a little at a time, until it is absorbed and the stuffing reaches the desired consistency (all a matter of taste, really; you may need more or less stock).

Cool to use as an actual stuffing, or put in a shallow buttered casserole and bake about 1/2 hour at 350°f. until crisp and crusty on top to serve as a side dish.

Makes enough to stuff a 12-15 pound turkey or serve 6-8 as a side dish.

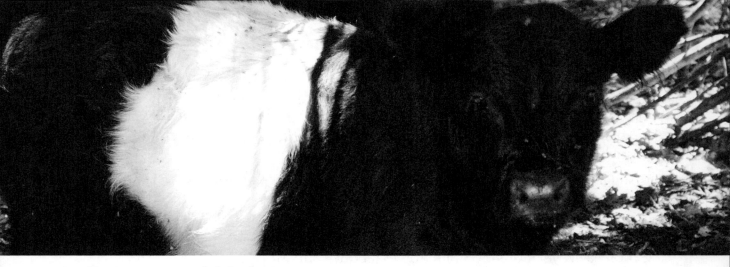

Organized Holsteins

Grass-fed Belted Galloways, Dennis Bires and Keetonville Farm.

CLAREMORE, OK – William Paul Winchester called it "the most pleasant life imaginable" in his 1995 memoir entitled *A Very Small Farm*, and that book had a great influence on Dennis Bires.

Bires is a professor of law at the University of Tulsa. He and his wife, Marian, have built that most pleasant life on twenty acres near Claremore, about thirty minutes north of Tulsa. Visiting them on a warm summer afternoon in 2004, the first thing I noticed was how much their animals are a part of the family. I had just sat down at their kitchen table with a glass of iced tea when one of the horses poked her head in the window to size-up the visitor. My move for my camera was too sudden for her though, and she trotted off to the grassy fields by the front gate before I could get the Mr. Ed photo I had hoped for.

The picturesque farm sits atop a ridge line overlooking Claremore, with grazing pasture interspersed with stands of oak, hickory and cedar. Near the house, a well-built chicken coop houses Australorps for meat and New Hampshires for laying. Both are chicken breeds registered with the American Livestock Breeds Conservancy (ALBC), a Pittsboro, North Carolina, organization that is working to protect over one hundred rare breeds of livestock from extinction, and the first American winner of the Slow Food Award for Biodiversity. Bires is a longstanding member.

We had a little further to walk to see the real reason I visited that day. Through one stand of cedars, across a pasture to another, we found Bires' small herd of Belted Galloway cattle. The Galloway is an ancient breed, dating back into the mists of history in the Scottish lowlands. It is not as endangered as its cousin, the Ancient White Park, but it is in more jeopardy than another Scottish relative, the Highland. The ALBC places the Galloway on its "Watch" list, which according to their Conservation Priority List parameters, means there are "fewer than 2500 annual registrations in the United States and estimated fewer than 10,000 global population. Also included are breeds with genetic or numerical concerns or limited geographic distribution."

Bires' cattle are called Belted Galloways because of their unique markings. My daughter says they look like an Oreo cookie – black at each end with a stripe, or belt of white around the middle. I have an uncle who calls them simply "organized Holsteins."

The great advantage of the Galloway lies in its self-sufficiency and the wonderful meat it produces on an all-grass diet. There is no need to "finish" them on corn to add fat because these naturally lean cattle can produce marvelous flavor in a 600-750-pound animal with far less fat than industrially processed feedlot cattle. Galloways care for themselves, calve easily, and those calves are up and milking very quickly. They can graze happily on many kinds of pasture that would starve an Angus, weedy and dry patches that some cattle wouldn't know what to do with.

Some have told me that they don't like the flavor of grass-fed beef. When I ask them to elaborate, most cannot. The few that can, speak of a "gaminess" and a "toughness," but I simply don't find those qualities in Keetonville Farm grass-fed Galloways. Of course, as with all beef, it is important to cook it properly – steaks to no more than medium rare and stew cuts simmered for a good long time – this will alleviate any textural issues. The flavor is not gamey (though gamey is not necessarily a bad thing); rather it is more intense – it tastes more, not different.

The Bireses keep the meat they need and sell the rest to friends and neighbors. It is all processed at a nearby state-inspected locker. They usually harvest them in June or July, since that is when the grass is at its best. Later in the summer all of Oklahoma dries into a uniform beige, and the greener, sweeter grass leaves of late spring leave the meat tasting sweet.

At first, Marian was wary of eating the animals they were raising (an attitude I've seen a lot of in my travels), but when their young bull broke through its fence three times in the first week it was at the farm, she said "I'm not sure I want to eat it, but I sure want to kill it!" Today many of the fans of humanely raised, pasture fed meat throughout the area are glad she and Dennis do what they do, and do it so well.

Grass-fed Belted Galloway Pot Roast

Once upon a time, recipes did not look like they do today, with a list of ingredients followed by a procedure. In fact, the great Auguste Escoffier, father of modern French cuisine, wrote all his recipes in simple prose, expecting the user to know the terms and techniques he included.

Here is Dennis Bires' recipe for pot roast, exactly as he related it to me. It is surprisingly easy to follow, as long as you read through it once before starting, as you should with any recipe.

Perfect for Chuck Roast, Arm Roast, Rump Roast
1. Salt and pepper meat to taste.
2. Heat several tablespoons of olive oil, or any other cooking oil, in a large covered pot or Dutch oven on medium high heat.
3. Brown all sides of meat in the hot oil, holding meat with forks or tongs to brown edges and ends for almost a minute each.
4. Add an inch or two of water, beef stock, cheap red wine, or any combination thereof to the pot, to submerge at least a third of the roast. Do not use a rack under meat.
5. Add cut-up onion and cut-up or minced garlic cloves – the more the better. Add a bit of your favorite herbs, for example, parsley, sage, rosemary, and thyme.
6. Cover tightly, and cook in preheated 325° oven for at least 2½ hours – until meat is falling off the bone. Turning and basting are not necessary. This can all be done on the stovetop too, at a simmer for the same length of time.
7. Check roast every half hour, adding liquid if necessary to maintain level. Allow cooking aroma to permeate house.
8. If desired, throw in cut-up potatoes, carrots, and/or celery for the last hour of cooking.
9. Remove roast and vegetables to serving platter. Put liquid into serving dish or boat to pour on each serving, or thicken in pot to make gravy.
10. If no potatoes were added to pot, have a large dish of mashed potatoes – extra large if serving children.

The Realization of a Dream
Simone Delaty's Plain and Simple.

WELLMAN, IA – I did not understand the paintings of Iowa native Grant Wood (he of the *American Gothic* fame) until I spent some time getting to know Simone Delaty's farm. Standing next to her brick oven, looking over the rolling hills of southeast Iowa with its hundred shades of green, you can begin to see what Wood was trying to convey. There is such a tranquil beauty to this place that you cannot resist connecting in a very personal way to the land itself. It was something akin to this feeling that brought Simone here twenty years ago, and it is why she is still here caring for the land.

Simone is not a native of this place. She arrived here through a series of coincidences that so often occur in this modern age, leading her from her home in Limousin, in central France, by way of Buffalo, New York, and Bowling Green, Ohio, to what became a twenty-eight-year career teaching French literature and related topics at the University of Iowa. Ten years before her retirement in 1996, she bought a piece of land about twenty-five minutes southeast of Iowa City, and set about making it into an organic farm. Slowly, through a lot of trial and error, she has built a paradise on the prairie that attracts people from hundreds and even thousands of miles away, just to have one meal with Simone.

What Simone has built is a farm and much more. It is the land that keeps her here, and it is what she does with the land that attracts so many people. Her vegetable and flower gardens are meticulously cared for, yielding the bounty she uses to contribute to Local Harvest CSA (see below) and to produce delightful private dinners throughout the season on her screened-in porch. Her orchard supplies apples, pears, and a variety of currants and nectarines for scrumptious desserts. Eggs are provided by her flock of Rhode Island Red and Barred Rock chickens. A pair of geese and their new goslings keep the chickens company.

Though her dinners were already successful, they got a tremendous boost in 2001 thanks to a visit by Rita Braver and the CBS *Sunday Morning* news crew. They had been working on a feature about the Slow Food Movement for their weekly show. When Slow Food USA's then-Executive Director Patrick Martins mentioned to Braver that Slow Food was far more than a "bi-coastal" movement, that we had Convivia in places like Chattanooga and Iowa City, she was intrigued. The CBS crew spent a weekend with the Iowa City convivium, visiting farms like Jordan Creek Bison Ranch and Simone's. When the segment aired in May of that year, Braver declared Simone "the reigning queen of Slow Food in Iowa," a crown she still wears.

That kind of exposure is hard to prepare for. The flood of inquiries that resulted from the CBS piece has helped to make it so that Simone's private dinners are sold out well in advance. If you would like to reserve a spot, you must call two to three months in advance, or even longer. By July, she's booked solid for the rest of the year. To accommodate those who do not wish to gather a large group on their own, Simone has begun a series of *table d'hote* dinners, once a month on Monday evenings. For these you can make reservations on your own or with a small group, and meet new people who share a love of great food. These too often sell out. Make your reservations at her website: www.simoneplainandsimple.com.

Simone calls what she does "Plain and Simple" because that's what it is – simple farmhouse cooking made with generations of French technique. Most of the dinners Simone prepares are rustic French fare, like her delectable cassoulet, made with almost exclusively local seasonal products. Those she does not raise herself she obtains from her friends and neighbors. She also has a love of Moroccan cuisine (her tagine, a classic Moroccan casserole, is renowned) and makes a variety of authentic pizzas and country breads in her wood-fired oven.

At Simone's you can understand the idea of placeness. The food is fabulous not just because of Simone's considerable culinary talent – which she learned at her aunt's and grandmother's apron strings – but because the food is literally garden fresh. "You have to do so little to food when it's a great product," she says.

Despite their success, the dinners are not the sole focus of her work. Along with Susan Jutz of ZJ Farm in Solon, Simone has helped to build the largest and most successful Community Supported Agriculture (CSA) organization in the area. Through Local Harvest CSA, community members receive fresh eggs, flowers, and wood-fired bread from Simone as well as fresh seasonal produce from ZJ Farm.

CSAs originated in Japan, where they are called *teikei*. Loosely translated, this means "food with the farmer's face." The idea is that local families pay a set amount in advance of the season and then receive fresh local produce once a week all season long, very like a subscription. The 140 families Local Harvest serves, and the close relationship with Susan, have become central to Simone's efforts.

It was this CSA that gave rise to Local Foods Connection, which is discussed later, and now Simone and Susan are creating an educational system with workshops specifically designed for grade school, high school, and college kids in an effort to reconnect the youth of Iowa to the land that made Iowa great.

"I am here to take care of this place," Simone says, "it's very satisfying." One would expect no less of any benevolent monarch, and this Queen of Slow Food in Iowa is indeed a munificent caretaker in this small corner of the world.

Vive la reine!

Soupe au Potiron (Pumpkin Soup)

In September and October, many of Simone's guests are treated to this harvest delight, which she serves from the natural "bowl" of a hollowed-out Rouge Vif d'Etampes or Potimarron pumpkin, what Americans call the "Cinderella" pumpkin (the low, broad kind). Also, she refers to something called *quatre epices*, or "four spices." It is roughly equal parts of ground pepper (white, black, or both), cloves, nutmeg and ginger. Some variations of the mix use allspice instead of pepper, or cinnamon in place of ginger.

This soup is pretty tasty cold, but to really appreciate it, serve it piping hot, outdoors, when there is just the barest nip of autumn in the air and perhaps someone burning leaves nearby.

2 medium onions
3 pound slice of pumpkin
2 garlic cloves
4 tablespoons olive oil
2 slices crusty bread, toasted
3 cups milk
3 cups heavy cream
3 cups water
Salt and white pepper to taste
A pinch or two of quatre epices
1 ½ ounces butter
Chervil or chives for decoration

Procedure

Peel and finely chop onions and garlic. Peel the pumpkin, remove all the "threads" in the inside, and rinse under cold water. Dice into small pieces. In a large heavy pot heat the olive oil and sauté onions, garlic, and pumpkin for 5 minutes on a low flame.

Remove crust from the toasted bread and set aside for other uses. Shred the bread directly in the pot on top of pumpkin and onions. Then add milk, cream and water. Add salt, pepper and quatre epices to taste. Cover the pot and let the soup simmer for 20 minutes. On a low flame add the butter cut up in small pieces. Test seasoning again and adjust if needed.

If you want texture do not mix soup further. Sometimes for a rustic appearance, Simone does not shred the bread but leaves the crusty slices at bottom of pan and transfers them to the tureen when serving. For a smooth texture, use a blender or food processor. Decorate with sprigs of chervil or a few chives.

Serves 8-12

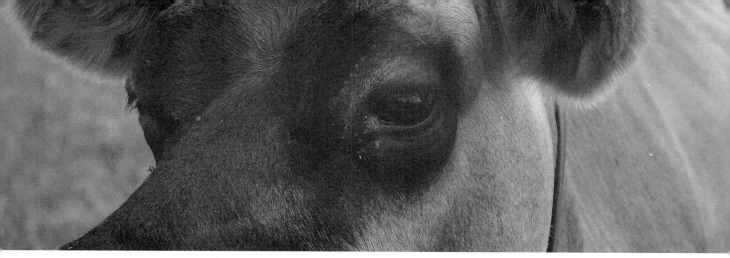

Got Raw Milk?

Debbie & Mark Apple and the Apple Family Farm.

MCCORDSVILLE, IN – A hidden debate has smoldered for quite some time over the benefits and/or dangers of raw (unpasteurized) milk and milk products. Rarely, however, will you see this argument take place in the halls of Congress or in the major media. More often, you'll see it played out at a small family farm, where bureaucrats will deliver a "Cease and Desist" order when they believe that someone may be selling fresh, raw milk.

Of course, their intentions are honorable. County health departments and state animal health boards are concerned about the dangers of food borne illness, and there is no doubt that pasteurization kills nearly all of the potential pathogens that might be found in milk. Unfortunately, it also kills much of the nutritive value of the milk and many beneficial microorganisms, which is why most commercial milk needs to be "fortified" with additional vitamins. It is this ultrasterilized view of how our food system should work that often reduces the body's ability to create its own natural antibodies, exposing us to the risk of other diseases. This, combined with the growing problem of antibiotic resistance caused in part by the antibiotics in our food, is creating real problems. Nonetheless a government's purpose is to serve and protect the people.

So what is a person, who does not wish for the government to choose her food, left to do?

Simple: own a cow.

Okay, it is true that finding a place in your suburban townhouse to board a cow may prove problematic, but Debbie and Mark Apple have a solution, and more than fifty families in the McCordsville, Indiana, area (northeast of Indianapolis) enjoy fresh, wholesome, raw milk as a result. The fact is that if you own the cow, you own the milk, and it does not matter where that cow is or who does the milking

The Apple Family farm has been in Mark's family since the 1930s. Besides the dairy cows, the Apples raise chickens, sheep, and beef, all of it without the use of chemicals, hormones, or subtherapeutic antibiotics. Most of the animals are rare breeds, because Debbie has an intense focus on biodiversity. Among the sheep are eleven rare, purebred Cotswold sheep. There are only about one thousand left in the US and about five thousand worldwide.

It was the sheep that brought the Apples back to the family farmstead, as well as Debbie's interest in a "simpler life" inspired by her fascination with a beautiful and intricate pair of hand-woven farmhouse curtains she saw in a museum. What sort of simpler life, she wondered, had made it possible for someone to have the time to take such care?

Now they like to say that they are grass farmers and the sheep are the harvesting equipment. "The nice thing about this arrangement is that we don't have to paint and wax the sheep in the winter and we get more sheep every spring. It must be something in the water. Not even the most expensive baler does that!"

Owning your very own cow can seem a little pricey at first, but when you divide it among a few families, and perhaps make your own butter and cheese, you will have loads of healthful, delicious dairy product for the life of the cow. Shares in a cow at the Apple Family Farm can be split as many as twenty ways, so the price quickly becomes reasonable.

A note about the taste. I must confess that my children had some difficulty with raw milk from a farm closer to home, in Iowa. But it was not a health issue nor even a flavor issue and actually had more to do with the lack of homogenization than with the lack of pasteurization. "It has chunks in it!" my daughter would scream. Those "chunks" were actually globules of milk fat from the cream that had risen to the top rather than being emulsified into the milk below (that's what homogenization does). Not bad, not bad tasting, just a little weird for kids who had previously only known the typical mass-produced variety. Just shake it before you serve it.

Another thing that concerns some is the flavor of milk from cows that were grass-fed or "pastured" rather than force-fed corn – something cows are not built to digest. Very much like the Bires' beef, the milk from Apple Family Farm has a much richer, much bigger, frankly much better flavor than the watered-down variety to which we've become accustomed. Personally, I like the difference and consider it to be not unlike the fact that not all wine tastes the same.

Corn feeding serves a secondary use in the dairy industry, by the way. It fattens the cows, and the number one purchaser of expired (no longer milking) cows is the McDonald's Corporation.

Still, the concerns over food borne illness linger. The USDA's Food Safety Research Information Office states on its website that: "raw (unpasteurized) milk has been associated with illness caused by microorganisms such as Listeria, Campylobacter, Yersinia, Salmonella,

Staphylococcus, and Escherichia coli" – that's the infamous e-Coli 0157:H7 you hear so much about these days. The proponents of raw milk argue that it is precisely the consumption of the pasteurized milk and other "sterilized" food products that has left us susceptible to these pathogens. A large portion of the strength of the immune system lies in the variety of bacteria living in the intestinal tracts of all of us that help our bodies build natural immunities. Raw milk, say its advocates, actually feeds and seeds those bacteria, literally increasing rather than decreasing your immune system strength.

Keep in mind that "raw milk" and "organic milk" are not necessarily the same thing. Milk can be one, the other or both. The primary positive attribute of organic when it comes to milk is the absence of Bovine Growth Hormone (BGH), which some studies have found to be dangerous for human consumption.

What Debbie and Mark Apple are doing is not some 1960s hippie culture back-to-the-land movement. It is an honest attempt to provide wholesome goodness for their neighbors and their family, something they feel can only be done with passionate respect for the animals and the land.

Rosemary, Lemon & Garlic Leg of Lamb with Roasted Potatoes

The mass-produced lamb from California or New Zealand simply is no comparison to the richness of flavor and aroma of one of Debbie and Mark's pastured spring lambs. Here's the way Debbie likes to prepare lamb for her own family.

2 large lemons, zest of 1 removed in strips with a vegetable peeler
1/4 cup fresh rosemary leaves
3 large garlic cloves
2 tablespoons olive oil
2 teaspoons fresh lemon juice
1/2 teaspoon salt
a 7-pound leg of lamb (ask butcher to remove pelvic bone and tie lamb
   for easier carving)
2 1/2 pounds small red potatoes
3 tablespoons minced fresh chives

Preheat oven to 350°

Cut off and discard pith from zested lemons. In a saucepan of boiling water blanch zest 1 minute and drain in a colander. Cut each lemon crosswise into 6 slices.

In a small food processor blend rosemary, garlic, zest, 1 tablespoon oil, lemon juice, and salt until mixture is chopped fine.

With tip of a small sharp knife cut small slits all over lamb and rub the rosemary mixture over lamb, rubbing into slits. Arrange lemon slices in middle of a large roasting pan and place lamb on them. Roast lamb in middle of oven 45 minutes.

Quarter potatoes and in a saucepan cover with salted cold water by 1 inch. Bring water to a boil and cook potatoes, covered, 5 minutes. Drain potatoes in colander and in a bowl toss with remaining tablespoon oil. Arrange potatoes around lamb and sprinkle with salt and pepper to taste.

Roast lamb and potatoes, stirring potatoes occasionally, an additional 55 minutes, or until a meat thermometer registers 130°F. for medium-rare. Transfer lamb to a cutting board and let stand 15 minutes. Increase temperature to 500°F. and roast potatoes and lemons in one layer 5 to 10 minutes more, or until golden.

Transfer potatoes and lemons with a slotted spoon to bowl and toss with chives. Transfer potato mixture to a platter.

Remove the sting that ties the leg together and serve, sliced thin across grain, with potatoes, garnished with rosemary and lemon wedges.

Makes 6-8 healthy servings.

The Complexities of Simplicity

Doug and Krista Dittman and Branched Oak Farm.

RAYMOND, NE – When she married him, he lived in what he called his bachelor pad, a true little house on the prairie. About 15 by 15 feet, it had one room on the ground level and a loft above. The new Mrs. Dittman concluded that they would need more room, and that is when Mr. Dittman started building. He's not done yet.

Their life since has been a series of adaptations: adding on to the small red brick cottage until it was a large family home; switching to a smaller, stockier breed of Angus cattle; adding seven Jersey cows for milking; modernizing the dairy; and adapting to suit local, state, and federal health regulations. That last one has proven to be the most challenging.

Doug and Krista Dittman's idea, all along, has been a very simple one. "I would just like to supply food for the neighborhood – just food sold to people," Doug said to me on one stifling July afternoon as we toured his unusual farm. It really isn't any more complicated than that, though some of the regulations he's had to deal with have made it harder.

Fortunately, unlike the troubles faced by Debbie and Mark Apple, it is legal to sell raw milk direct to the public in Nebraska, but only on the farm where it originates. The Dittmans began selling milk from their grass-fed Jerseys along with beef from the Angus cattle, some eggs from a small flock of laying hens, and the occasional broiler chicken. All this was in the original cottage at one end of the house Doug had built.

For the benefit of his customers, and to facilitate their anticipated cheesemaking operation, he built a new dairy with a small store attached, and a windowed door to allow a view of the milking room. This store, it would later be revealed, would require a convenience store license, so the Dittmans applied and received one. That's when the Law of Unintended Consequences began to take hold. The store passed its county health inspection without difficulty, but state officials said the raw milk could not be sold in a convenience store.

Whether they are doing it intentionally or not (how conspiratorial they are often appears to depend on how cynical you are, it seems), the government regulations in the world of agriculture are designed for the lowest common denominator. They assume that the consumer is a dolt, because it is true that some are, and design laws to protect them from themselves. The Unintended Consequences of this always benefit large corporate interests over those of the small, independent farmer or food producer.

The larger corporations can afford to make hypersanitized modifications to their facilities. The little guy cannot.

Wendell Berry, the farmer, poet and activist, once wrote, "Eating is an agricultural act." It is also a political act, a moral act, and a philosophical, even religious act. Each time we take a bite of food, each time we wash it down with a beverage, we are making a choice about who we are and about the way we want the world our children live in to be.

The Dittman's cows and chickens are very happy. They've never seen a veterinarian, have never needed to. Doug told me that he once heard a large animal veterinarian say, "If it weren't for big corporate agriculture and those big feed lots, I'd be out of a job." Vets have nothing to do on farms where the livestock is healthy and self-sufficient.

Small and middle-sized farms have quite a challenge when they try to produce simple food rather than commodities in this modern, mechanized era. Doug and Krista persevere, though, on their bucolic little farm in eastern Nebraska, with their kids, their dog, and many happy cows and chickens. They are working through the bureaucracy that makes selling real food a challenge and living the life they want, "just selling food to people."

Meat and Spinach Manicotti

Krista adapted this recipe from one she first found in Joanna White's *Recipes For Yogurt Cheese*. When she started making it with her own homemade yogurt (from her own pastured cows), it instantly became a family favorite. Krista said, "I've even substituted chard and bok choy for the spinach, and my boys still eat it!"

> 1 pound ground meat (use beef, lamb, or turkey)
> 1 medium yellow onion, minced
> ½ cup Yogurt cheese (1 cup pain yogurt drained through cheesecloth),
>   or homemade ricotta (see previous recipe)
> ½ cup grated Parmigiano Reggiano (genuine Parmesan) cheese
> 3 beaten eggs
> ¾ cup fresh breadcrumbs
> 1 tablespoon each fresh parsley, basil, and oregano, chopped
> Kosher salt and fresh cracked black pepper, to taste
> 1 cup steamed, chopped spinach
> 1 8 ounce package dry manicotti, cooked according to package directions
> 3 cups homemade marinara sauce
> ½ cup grated mozzarella

Preheat oven to 375°

In a large sauté pan, brown the ground meat with the onion (use a little olive oil for the leaner meats). Allow to cool, then mix with the yogurt cheese or ricotta, Parmigiano, eggs, breadcrumbs, herbs, salt, pepper, and spinach. Stuff the manicotti with this filling (a pastry bag works best, but a spoon and your fingers will suffice). Place in a lightly oiled 9-inch casserole, then cover with the sauce and grated mozzarella.

Bake, covered, for 25 minutes. If you like the cheese browned, uncover and cook a further 10 minutes or to desired doneness.

Allow to rest 10 minutes, then portion and serve. Serves 4-6

Bananas, Bees and Bambi

Honey Hill Farm Fallow Deer.

GUTHRIE, OK – There is a small slice of heaven on the Oklahoma prairie, just across the clay-red Cimarron River from Guthrie, about an hour north of Oklahoma City. Here Jerry and JoAnn Logan have built an unusual farm. Unusual because rather than the acres of ubiquitous wheat or livestock, the Logans have 170 free range chickens, 140 beehives, a dozen or so banana trees (yes, I said banana trees), and 350 head of fallow deer.

Each spring Jerry and JoAnn plant the banana trees around the patio, overlooking a lovely pond, and each fall they move them back to his hothouse. The trees do very well, and have even fruited.

The bees and the deer are the primary work of the farm. A retired secondary school teacher, Jerry has kept bees for more than thirty years and is the president of the Oklahoma Beekeepers' Association. He keeps his hives on his farm and on surrounding farms, as far away as Newcastle (fifty miles south), where they feed on wild flowers, alfalfa, vetch and clover. Jerry's Honey House bottling facility is a state- and county-inspected facility in nearby Edmond. The honey is available from local stores and at select area restaurants, as well as through the Oklahoma Food Cooperative .

Jerry has had no trouble yet with the honey bee mite that is wiping out hives nationwide, but fears his luck may run out soon. Research into controlling the Varroa mite is ongoing, and Jerry knows that early detection of low levels of mite infestations is key to its successful management. Colony Collapse Disorder is the newest threat and no one quite knows what to do about this yet.

It was seeing his deer that had me particularly entranced. The Logans maintain Oklahoma's first USDA accredited fallow herd in eleven five-to-fifteen-acre paddocks, using only five or six of the paddocks at a time. This rotational grazing method keeps the soil, and therefore the grass that sustains the herd, healthy and vibrant. The paddocks are each surrounded by six-foot post and wire fences, which have electrical wires running along the outside bottom edge to discourage predators. This method is effective enough that the Logans are confident leaving the young to be raised naturally by the mother does, who are excellent parents.

All of the paddocks are interconnected, and if need be, Jerry can herd all 350 head into a series of raceways and into the barn in about thirty minutes, by himself, using an ordinary tractor. Actually, make that 348, because Honey Hill Farm has two particularly spry Mesopotamian bucks, and it requires quite a few people, and some careful strategic planning to convince the young princes to do anything they don't want to do. When facing 350 pounds of very agile, very frightened meat attached to a pair of two-foot antlers, caution is indeed the watchword.

Fallows are a European and Eurasian breed, raised and hunted since before the time of the Greeks. The Romans spread them throughout the continent and Britain, where later the Normans and subsequent royals raised them for hunting. The penalty for poaching them was death.

The deer feed primarily on a diet of native grasses and clover, which is supplemented in the winter with homegrown hay and a feed mix of sunflower, soy and corn. They do not receive any antibiotics or hormones and live largely independently. Each paddock has a llama in it. Jerry had heard that the llamas were effective at keeping the coyotes away. It turned out not to be true, but Jerry kept the llamas anyway. They are pretty to look at after all.

The llamas were the first to eat when Jerry called the deer close for me to see by pouring some feed mix in a trough in one of the paddocks. His presence didn't seem to bother the llamas or the deer, but they were quite skittish around me, never getting closer than about twenty feet. The camera seemed to frighten them as well, or perhaps it was just the motion of my arms. Any movement they interpreted as hostile inspired the whole herd to move in perfect unison, like a school of fish, in seeming lockstep toward the far end of the paddock.

Honey Hill Farm venison is available almost exclusively to area restaurants like the Coach House, the Metro, and the Museum Café, all in Oklahoma City. The only other way to get it is to join the Oklahoma Food Co-op (www.oklahomafood.org). Robert Waldrop and the Co-op folks had to jump through an awful lot of bureaucratic hoops to be able to provide meat to their members. Distribution day, which occurs once a month for the fast-growing group, is complicated by the strict requirements they must follow. Nonetheless, the dozen or so volunteers cheerfully sanitize the insulated coolers by hand, sort and resort the orders dropped off all morning by participating farmers, then pack everything on dry ice to keep it cold on its way to Tulsa, Norman, and many other distribution points throughout the Sooner state.

When I visited, Jerry had driven down to the First Nazarene Church on the Northwest Expressway in Oklahoma City with two coolers, one full of honey and honeycombs, the other with fallow jerky, ground venison and shoulder roast. Along with dozens of other farmers and artisan food producers, he checked in his product, and the co-op volunteers took over from there, seeing to it that the fresh food would arrive promptly to its hundreds of members.

Thanks to the hard work of these volunteers, and of visionary farmers like Jerry and JoAnn Logan, Oklahomans are relishing the rich flavor of farm-raised fallow deer and clover honey all year long. As Robert Waldrop likes to say, "Y'all bon appétit, you hear?"

Rosemary Venison

Here is some Slow Food that actually does use a slow cooker. JoAnn says this was originally a simple beef dish that she adapted to suit the venison so long ago she doesn't remember when.

> 2 ½ pounds venison, shoulder or round, diced in 1-inch cubes (note: it's easiest to dice when it is partially frozen)
> 1 cup dry red wine
> ½ cup tomato puree
> ¼ cup red wine vinegar
> 4 tablespoons Worcestershire sauce
> 1 tablespoon fresh rosemary, destemmed and chopped
> 1 teaspoon dry mustard
> 1 clove fresh garlic, sliced paper thin
> Salt and cracked black pepper to taste

Brown the venison in a large skillet, in small batches so as not to overcrowd the pan. Note that Cooking too much at once will cause the meat to trap moisture, steaming rather tan browning the meat. Without the caramelization of browning, you lose a great deal of sweetness. When all the meat is browned, deglaze the pan by pouring in the red wine – this loosens the caramelized bits stuck to the pan - then pour this glaze and all the meat into a slow cooker.

Combine the tomato puree, vinegar, Worcestershire, rosemary, mustard, and garlic well and pour into the cooker. Turn to low setting and cook for 2-3 hours, or until the meat is quite tender. Adjust seasoning to taste with salt and fresh cracked black pepper, adding additional fresh rosemary if desired.

Serve over rice, garnished with a rosemary sprig. Serves 4-6 as an entrée.

A Boy's Best Friend Is his Goat

Ken, Jennifer and Peter Muno, Tragopogon Dubius
& Goatsbeard Artisanal Cheeses.

HARRISBURG, MO – Ken and Jennifer Muno met when they were both employees of the famous Zingerman's Delicatessen on Detroit Street in Ann Arbor, Michigan. There they developed a love for each other and a love for cheese. Today, that love has led to the creation of Goatsbeard Farm, in the rolling hills above the Missouri River outside Columbia, where they make marvelous artisanal cheeses from the milk of forty very happy goats, all crosses between Nubian, Saanen and Alpine breeds.

Goatsbeard Farm takes its name not, as you may expect, from a resident Billy goat but rather from a local wildflower, the *Tragopogon dubius*, commonly known as goatsbeard. A relative of the daisy, it is one of the many indigenous wild plants that the Muno's goats feast on in their wide-open pastures. Free range feeding like this is a part of the Muno's commitment to sustainability, and the source of the unique flavors of their cheese.

Ken is the primary cheesemaker, Jenn cares for the goats, and their son, Peter – five years old when I visited in 2005, is learning to feed and herd them. He is very effective with the young kids, who follow him as though he were the Pied Piper. If you haven't had the opportunity to see small children with baby goats, you really must avail yourself next spring. It is quite a sight.

The goats are milked twice a day from March through December, then are given a break in January and February as they prepare to kid. This is in keeping with their natural cycle, and it yields about a gallon of milk per goat each day. This translates to roughly 12,000 gallons per year. It may sound like a lot, but it is actually miniscule compared to the output of commercial dairies.

All the milk is used to make the six cheeses Goatsbeard Farm produces. The fresh goat cheese, which is pasteurized, is available in rounds and in tubs. This is the one that shows the "placeness" of their cheese. Two soft-ripened cheeses, Prairie Bloom and Missouri Moon, both have delicate blooms and creamy, delicate centers. The Franklin Island feta is made in the Bulgarian style (a denser, sharper style which I prefer to the Greek) and is stored in a slightly salty brine.

Ken makes two raw milk cheeses. The "Walloon" is a hard cheese with a nutlike flavor. It slices and grates well, and is a delicious alternative to Parmigiano. The rich, sharp Moniteau Blue won consecutive blue ribbons at the 2002 and 2003 Missouri Sate Fair, and is one of many delicious new blues coming from the Heartland these days.

The raw milk cheeses are of special interest to the Slow Food Movement. In 2003, Slow Food USA formed the American Raw Milk Farmstead Cheese Consortium as a way to support the artisans who were making these delightful cheeses, on their farm, with their own milk using old world, traditional methods.

In 2004, when the American Raw Milk Cheeses were sampled, at Slow Food's biennial flagship event, the Salone del Gusto, the reaction was one of unanimous amazement. "Si? Americano? In tutto Americano?!" Everyone was delighted with the high quality and excellent craftsmanship of the American cheeses, which stood proudly alongside some of the best and most storied in the world. It was a treat to show the Europeans that we Americans can produce more than Velveeta® and Cheez Whiz®.

The Munos make just this sort of world-class cheese. They are vigilant in their guardianship of the land and the flock, and care deeply about their product, their family and their community. Proving once again that if it's raised with care, prepared with passion and served with love, then the result is sure to please.

Niçoise Tart with Goat Cheese

Martha Folk, Goatsbeard Farm and Slow Food Katy Trail, Harrisburg, MO

This recipe, created by Martha Folk (Jennifer's mom) uses a frozen puff pastry dough. Of course fresh puff dough is far better, but even fanatics for authenticity like myself recognize that the time and expertise needed to make homemade puff pastry dough are beyond the reach of most home cooks. By all means though, make it if you can, or ask a local bakery to prepare some for you.

> 2 tablespoons olive oil, plus a little extra for drizzling
> 1 cup red onion, sliced
> Salt and fresh cracked black pepper to taste
> 1 8-inch by 10-inch sheet frozen puff pastry
> ½ cup sun dried tomato paste or basil pesto
> 1 4-ounce round Goatsbeard Farm fresh goat cheese
> 2 or 3 heirloom tomatoes, sliced
> ½ cup Niçoise olives, halved and pitted
> 3 tablespoons chopped fresh herbs: basil and/or thyme
> 1 egg yolk, beaten with a dash of water

Preheat oven to 425°

Heat olive oil over medium flame, then add onion. Reduce to medium-low and cook slowly, stirring occasionally, until onion is caramelized, about 30 minutes. Season with salt and fresh cracked black pepper.

Lay the puff pastry on a cookie sheet or baking stone. With a sharp knife, score a center section approximately 1 inch from edge (don't cut all the way through). This will "puff" into a border for the tart. Spread the inner rectangle with tomato paste or pesto. Arrange cheese, tomatoes, olives, onions and herbs on top. Drizzle with additional olive oil. Brush outer frame of tart with egg yolk. Bake at 425° for 5 minutes, and then lower heat to 375° for about 10 minutes or until brown and bubbly.

Remove and let rest for 4 or 5 minutes before slicing, then serve immediately. Serves 4-6

A Vanishing Breed

How Kevin Powell is Saving the Mulefoot Hog.

STRAWBERRY POINT, IA – Iowa is the biggest pork producer in the US, but most of the hogs grown here are artificially inseminated, hormone and antibiotic-laden inmates confined in Concentrated Animal Feeding Operations known commonly as CAFOs or "hog lots." Quietly though, there are farmers who are resisting the pressure to join the meat processing multinationals. They are raising heritage breeds in deep beds and pasture, free to be happy pigs wallowing and rooting with their offspring as they do naturally, with no hormones or subtherapeutic antibiotics. One such grower is Kevin Powell, and the story of his Slow Food Ark registered Mulefoot hogs begins quite a long time ago.

Five centuries ago, Spanish explorers were populating the Atlantic and Gulf coasts, but not with people as much as with pigs. The swine brought over from Europe would be set free along the coasts of what became the Carolinas, Georgia, and Florida, to be harvested as needed when settlers arrived. Some of the descendants of those pigs can still be found running wild there. Most, though, were herded up by farmers and domesticated for food and trade in the newly burgeoning southern United States.

One of the popular practices was to keep hogs on small islands in rivers like the Mississippi and the Missouri. These islands worked as natural corrals, but they were very wet, and some breeds would develop foot rot. Through selective breeding techniques, one variety was developed without the pig's usual cloven hoof (a characteristic called "syndactylism"), thus seeming to help it avoid the bacteria that caused foot rot. These came to be known as mulefoots, and their hardiness combined with excellent flavor made them a very popular breed throughout the nineteenth and early twentieth centuries. It was rumored (though later disproved) that they were immune to hog cholera, and this added to their popularity among farmers. The National

Mulefoot Hog Record Association was organized in Indianapolis, Indiana, in January 1908, and by 1910 there were 235 breeders registered in the US.

When the Army Corps of Engineers banned the practice of corralling pigs on river islands – it had something to do with recreational use and people not liking pigs at their picnics – the popularity of this delicious breed declined. The mule-like hoof, meant for muddy riverbanks, did not fare well on the concrete floors of hog lots. Industrialization and a focus on a narrow genetic line of swine nearly decimated the breed.

In 1964 a man named R.M. Holliday of Louisiana, Missouri, took up the task of reestablishing this vanishing breed. He bought registered mulefoots from a wide area and created his own breeding herd. He sold some of his herd to Mark Fields, of Clark, Missouri, who enlisted the aid of the American Livestock Breeds Conservancy in rebuilding the Mulefoot registry. They in turn contacted Kent Whealy of the Seed Savers Exchange in Decorah, Iowa, who took them on behalf of the Institute for Biodiversity at Luther College.

Down the road in Strawberry Point, Kevin Powell was looking for a way to use his degree in animal science from Iowa State University on his family's fifty-four-year-old farm. Frustrated with the narrowing of the livestock gene pool, he became interested in diversity and what he calls ethical genetics. He found a way to make a difference with Whealy's herd of Mulefoots in 1998.

Powell now cares for a herd of 30 mulefoots and is the chairman of the National Mulefoot Hog Association. It is a very small association though, since the ALBC lists the Mulefoot as critically endangered, the rarest American breed of hog still in existence. Today there are fewer than 200 left in the world.

In 2005, the Mulefoot Hog boarded the Slow Food Ark. The Ark is one of three major endeavors of Slow Food USA to preserve, protect and promote foods that are in danger of extinction due to the industrial standardization of flavors in the food supply. To date, more than 250 indigenous American foods have been carefully catalogued in the Ark USA, joining the hundreds that are on the international Ark.

The mission is to preserve endangered tastes – and to celebrate them, by introducing them to the membership and then to the world, through media, public relations, and Slow Food events. In addition to the Ark, Slow Food USA also forms Presidia, or "active defenses" of certain products that can benefit from a more vigorous intervention to promote their well-being.

Through programs like these, and the tireless efforts of visionary farmers like Kevin Powell, Slow Food is protecting a world of flavors. When writer and farmer Wendell Berry famously said, "Eating is an agricultural act," he meant also that conversely, farming is a culinary act. Just as we, as consumers, should be keenly aware of the origins of our food and of the people involved, so too should the farmers be looking back along the food chain, toward an awareness that flavor and nutritional quality are of interrelated importance.

Hickory-Smoked Pork Shoulder with "Pig Pucker" Sauce

Barbecue is America's ultimate Slow Food. Made well, everything about it reflects the values of the movement – taking time, raising with care, serving with passion and joy – you just can't beat good 'Q.

I love all kinds of barbeque, but despite my heartland roots, when it comes to my favorite 'Q I always turn to my childhood summers spent in North Carolina. Now every region has its own style of fantastic barbecue, and the Heartland is no different (just ask the folks in Kansas City, Oklahoma City, Chicago, or Omaha). But for pure, decadent, lascivious eating pleasure it is darn tough to beat a North Carolina picnic.

Down there the 'Q is always pork (usually shoulder), always hickory smoke, and always served with a unique cider vinegar sauce called "Pig Pucker" that cuts through the fat and compliments the smoke with a sweet-hot tang.

I served this dish to the Slow Food USA Ark Committee in 2005 when the mulefoot hog was boarded onto the Ark, and of course I used some of Kevin Powell's marvelous pork. The process looks daunting at first but is actually quite simple. Most of the time involved is just waiting during the marinating and smoking processes.

> 1 whole, local pasture raised pork shoulder (also called a "butt"), 12 to 14
>   pounds with bone or 8 to 10 pounds without
> 3/4 cup brown sugar
> 1/4 cup smoked paprika
> 1/4 cup chopped fresh garlic
> 1/4 cup kosher salt
> 2 tablespoons freshly cracked black pepper
> 2 tablespoons cumin (preferably toasted whole and then ground fresh)
> 2 tablespoons fresh chopped sage (or 1 tablespoon dried)
> 1 teaspoon dry mustard
> 2 teaspoons fresh chopped thyme

36 hours before you are ready to serve, Mix all the dry ingredients and thoroughly coat the pork shoulder. Marinate in a plastic bag or covered bowl, refrigerated, for 24 hours.

About 12 hours before you are ready to serve, start some hardwood charcoal in your grill or smoker. Many now come with built in temperature gauges, and you'll want to maintain about 200-220° throughout the process. Soak plenty of hickory chips (about 10 pounds) in water for 1 hour, drain and add to fire as needed. More wood equals more smoke, which equals smokier flavor.

Cook the pork in this atmosphere, careful not to set it directly above the heat, for about 10 hours, or until the internal temperature is 180°. Stoke the fire as needed to maintain an even temperature. Remove and allow to rest 20 to 30 minutes. Pull the pork apart with a fork and serve by itself or on a bun, with your favorite slaw and Pig Pucker sauce

"Pig Pucker" Sauce

> 1 1/2 cups cider vinegar
> 3/4 cup water
> Sugar and salt to taste (start with about 2 tablespoons sugar and 1 tablespoon salt)
> 1 tablespoon dried hot red pepper flakes
> 1 small red onion, sliced as thinly as possible
> Cracked black pepper to taste (about 1/2 teaspoon)

Mix all ingredients until the sugar and salt dissolve, drizzle over the chopped pork, then pig out!

This sauce will keep for months in the refrigerator.

Happy Birds, Healthy Meat

Julie and Tim Walker of Greystone Farm.

FAYETTE, MO – The Katy Trail Convivium of Slow Food was founded in late 2003 by Bernadette Dryden and a group of concerned foodies and farmers in and around Columbia, Missouri. One of those farmers, Julie Walker, saw it as her opportunity to make more people aware of the importance of local, sustainably raised food.

At Greystone Farm, north of Columbia, Julie and her husband, Tim, raise chickens, turkeys, pigs and cattle for sale directly to the consumer. Their method of raising livestock is almost as old as farming itself, but it fell out of favor and was almost completely lost in this age of industrial agriculture. Today concerned farmers around the Heartland are reviving the idea of pastured livestock, allowing the animals to forage for their own food as much as possible and changing the pasture where they graze regularly. This provides a steady supply of fresh food and allows pastures to recover – preventing overgrazing which sustains the soil and therefore the habitat.

There are a number of ways to raise pastured poultry. The semi-intensive or yarding system is what you might imagine from Old McDonald's Farm: a permanent hen house that allows access to a fenced outdoor pen. The physical location of the pen is changed from time to time, allowing the land to recover. With a movable pen method, popularized by Virginia farmer and author Joel Salatin, one makes the whole system portable, keeping the birds in their floorless pens but towing the pens to different parts of the field.

The method the Walkers prefer for their turkeys and chickens is called day ranging. It is a sort of cross between the other two, where the chickens and turkeys are allowed free range inside a large electric-fenced paddock during the day and are enclosed in a weather-tight and predator-proof shelter at night. The weather is fairly easy to keep out, but the predators are always a challenge. Raccoons, possums, and hawks are a constant threat to Greystone

Farm's birds, digging under walls and even opening latched doors, but the Walkers learn from experience and almost always outwit the wily hunters.

The layers and broilers live on a diet of what they forage from the pasture, supplemented as needed with grains that are custom-mixed for them at a local feed mill. Chickens and turkeys must have both pasture and grain to gain weight steadily and lay eggs consistently.

The benefits of this method of raising poultry are numerous. It is better for the land and therefore better for the farm and the community around it. There are no lagoons of animal waste to pollute the air and groundwater because the waste all biodegrades naturally, fertilizing the land. The birds are humanely treated, unlike the chicken factories of the industrialized poultry world. In the end, all this makes for better tasting, more nutritious eggs and meat, which in turn allow the Walkers to ask a fair price for the birds. The people at the Fayette Farmers' Market, which the Walkers helped found, are more than willing to pay it.

Each bird provides a net profit of $2.50 to $3.00, compared to the pennies per bird that a farmer receives under contract to the big meat processors. The chickens and turkeys at Greystone Farm do not suffer this system, and so neither do the Walkers. Their Slow Food Ark USA–registered American Bronze turkeys command a high price in the fall, and people willingly pay it because they understand the quality of the meat, the work that goes into raising it, and the true, hidden costs of "cheap" food.

Julie hopes that Slow Food's Presidia projects, which provide an active defense to support and promote endangered foods and the people who produce them, might one day help to develop a system of custom-butchering plants for farms like hers. Right now Tim must drive the birds nearly 180 miles to Springfield to be processed in a licensed and inspected facility. The rising cost of gas has hit them hard. The landscaping work they do helps support the farm.

The Walkers keep at it, though, secure in the knowledge that they are doing the right thing for their birds, their farm, and their community.

Chicken on a Throne

Also known as Beer Can Chicken, this is a favorite trick of backyard grillmasters throughout the Heartland. Any beer in a can will do, but I usually use the Japanese beer Sapporo, because it comes in a tall steel can rather than aluminum. Some companies now make accessories for their grills that suit the purpose, but a beer can works fine.

Julie Walker says: "When roasting a pastured bird always use a meat thermometer to check for doneness instead of cooking by time, as pasture-raised chickens cook up faster because they don't sponge up water during processing like confinement chickens do. An overcooked bird is a wasted bird."

> 12-ounce can of your choice of beer
> 1/4 cup barbecue rub (Julie likes to use a Cajun blend, the kind with plenty of garlic and cayenne)
> 1 3 ½ - 4 ½ pound, 8-12 week old pasture-raised roasting chicken washed and blotted dry.

This recipe involves grilling a chicken using a method called indirect heat, that is, you should configure your fire so that it is hottest away from the food. On a charcoal grill, after the coals are well started, separate them into 2 mounds near the outer edge of the grill making sure there is enough room in the center for a drip pan directly under the chicken. Place grate on grill and chicken over beer can in drip pan in center of grate. Real hardwood charcoal (not briquettes) tastes best, however if you must use a gas grill with two burners, light one on high and cook chicken over other unlit one, turning the bird in the drip pan carefully as necessary for even cooking. Whether using a charcoal or a gas grill, keep grill covered while cooking to maintain heat at 350°

After setting grill for indirect cooking, open beer can and make two more holes in top of the can with an ice pick or churchkey. Use 1/4 of can to moisten breast area and internal cavity of chicken. Sprinkle 1 teaspoon of your rub in the neck cavity and two teaspoons in main cavity of chicken. Add 1tablespoon of your rub to open can of beer. Don't worry if it foams up. Season the outside of bird with remaining rub.

Place the beer can in the drip pan (a disposable aluminum one will do). Holding the chicken with the neck cavity upright, sit the bird down so that the main cavity fits over beer can. Pull chicken legs forward to form a tripod; hence the bird is sitting on the can.

Transfer the drip pan with the chicken to the grill away from intense heat. Roast the bird until nicely browned and cooked through (using your meat thermometer to make sure that internal temperature of chicken reaches 165° at the thigh and breast). Lift the bird off of the can, place it on platter and serve. Approximate cooking time is 1 3/4 hours. Yields 3 to 4 servings depending on size of bird.

Chief Executive Cogitator

Bill Leefers and Jordan Creek Bison Farm.

SOLON, IA – Doubtless you have heard the stories before. "Once they roamed the plains in herds of millions…. Their stampedes the sound of distant rolling thunder…. Callously slaughtered by European settlers to the point of extinction…." All of that is true, but today's story of the bison is one of hope and redemption, of conservation through consumption, and of a one-hundred-year-old movement to save an American icon.

It is also the story of three different Williams from Iowa. All three are closely intertwined with the fate of the bison, each in a different way.

Born in 1846 in what would become Scott County, Iowa, later that same year, William Cody would grow to be one of the most recognizable men in the world for his Wild West Show, his legendary marksmanship, and his use of that skill to kill (by his own estimate) some 4,200 bison in a little over a year to feed legions of railroad workers. At a ton apiece, that's some 8,000,000 pounds of meat. Buffalo Bill, as he came to be known, was as misunderstood by everyone as most celebrities still are to this day.

It is true that he killed hundreds of bison, but his kill was always used for meat, as opposed to the wasteful slaughter that decimated both the once-abundant herds and the Plains tribes who depended on them. Cody was a skilled scout for the U.S. cavalry, but respected the Natives enough to warn the U.S. government to never make a promise to the Indians that wouldn't be kept.

Cody was instrumental in expediting the westward expansion, yet he and the developers who built the town of Cody, Wyoming would also be instrumental in the creation of Yellowstone National Park.

The near-annihilation of the Bison herds in the late 1800s, which took their numbers from the millions to the hundreds in just a few decades, was the inspiration for another William to create a foundation to save the noble beast from extinction.

William Temple Hornaday, Sr., and his wife, Martha, followed the Mormon Trail westward from Indiana and settled in Eddyville, Iowa, with their two-year-old son William Jr. in 1856. That son would later attend nearby Oskaloosa College, and then go on to America's first land grant college, Iowa State University. He studied zoology and traveled the world honing his skills as a taxidermist. Later he would become the chief taxidermist for the United States National Museum (the cornerstone of the Smithsonian). His use of taxidermy to depict animals in their natural setting transformed the art. Hornaday played vital roles in the creation of both the Bronx and National Zoos.

After traveling to Montana to collect bison for the Smithsonian, Hornaday became keenly aware of the plight of the noble beast, and in 1905 he founded the American Bison Society. Estimates of the number of Bison in existence at that time ranged from 1,500 to as few as 300. Extinction seemed inevitable.

Enter a third William of Iowa. Bill Leefers is one of a growing number of farmers and ranchers throughout the Heartland utilizing the seemingly juxtaposed concepts of conservation and consumption.

Enticed from the workaday world of mortgage banking in 1996 by the romanticism of a buffalo herd, Leefers raises about one hundred head on his 110 acres near Solon, Iowa. They are part of the estimated 350,000 bison currently living in the U.S. and Canada, a remarkable recovery due mostly to the creation of a viable market for ranchers to sell the meat. "If you want to save the bison," Leefers says, "you need to eat it." Without the bison ranchers, the herd that once numbered in the tens of millions would be reduced to a curiosity in zoos and parks, or gone altogether.

Leefers' Bison roam paddocks ranging from two to ten acres, rotated to maintain the health of the soil and therefore the grass that the bison eat. They require far less work than conventional cattle because they take very good care of themselves. Leefers says there is less physical work but a lot more planning and thinking (thus his title, Chief Executive Cogitator). His bison need almost no veterinary care, save for an occasional worming, and receive no hormones or subtherapeutic antibiotics. Although this part of Iowa has seen a big influx of coyotes recently, they are not stupid enough to mess with a herd of bison, so predators are not an issue here.

Leefers harvests his bison at twenty-four to thirty months, far older than their domestic cattle counterparts. They are processed by a local, family-owned meat locker called Ruzicka's and sold to individuals and restaurants throughout the area (including mine). People love the meat for its deep, rich flavor and its amazing nutritional value. Perhaps its biggest selling point is that it has more protein, less fat and less cholesterol than boneless, skinless chicken breast.

A long time Slow Food member and a Terra Madre delegate, Bill Leefers understands the importance of sustainable farming practices and the traditions of the table. His meat has been featured at numerous Slow Food Iowa events and is likely to continue to be a mainstay of eastern Iowa menus, from diners to the fanciest bistros.

Once the pure majesty of the Heartland and source of sustenance to countless generations of Native Americans, then reduced to near extinction by unconscionable avarice, the bison is now well on the road to full recovery, thanks to visionary Heartland ranchers like Bill Leefers.

Devotay Albondigas

Devotay, my restaurant in Iowa City, is primarily a tapas bar. Since 1996, one tapa that has never left the seasonally changing menu is the albondigas, or meatballs. In the Spanish tradition, these would be made with beef, veal, and/or pork, but we have always used Bill Leefers' bison to great acclaim.

This recipe is for a crowd, but it scales well, so halve it or even quarter it at will.

1 onion, minced
2 tablespoons garlic, chopped
2 tablespoons olive oil
2 tablespoons salt
¼ cup herbs, chopped (At Devotay we use a mix of roughly equal parts parsley, thyme, oregano, basil and rosemary, all chopped together in a mix we've come to call cherb)
½ cup sherry
4 pounds ground bison
6 eggs
3 tablespoons Worcestershire sauce
Enough bread crumbs for desired consistency

Preheat oven to 375°

Sauté the onion and garlic in olive oil until tender with salt, herbs and garlic. Deglaze by adding sherry, then reduce liquid 50 percent by simmering, and cool.

Mix the bison with eggs and Worcestershire, then add cooked, cooled onions and breadcrumbs until proper consistency is reached. To test the consistency, portion with a sorbet-size scoop, and form into balls a little smaller than golf balls. If they hold up well, you have the right consistency. This can be affected by moisture content in the air, in the meat, or in the breadcrumbs, so it is always variable.

Form a small amount into a patty and fry it quickly on the stove top, then taste for seasoning and adjust to taste.

Portion the rest of the meat mixture just as you did for the consistency test, placing them on a parchment-lined cookie sheet, then bake about 15 minutes or until firm. Serve plain or mix with your favorite tomato sauce recipe.

ARTISANS

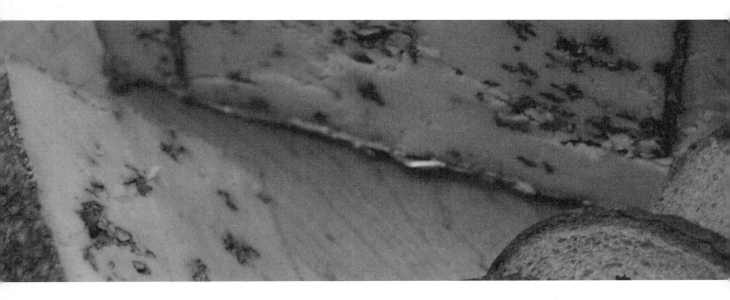

"There is scarcely anything in the world that some man cannot make a little worse, and sell a little more cheaply. The person who buys on price alone is this man's lawful prey."
-John Ruskin

Al Capone Drank Here

The Rebirth of Templeton Rye.

TEMPLETON, IA – It was the Jazz Age, a time of speakeasies, gangsters and bathtub whiskey. Railroad cars crossed the country carrying hobos and the occasional load of table grapes with stenciled warnings, "Caution: Grapes—Do Not Add Yeast or Fermentation Will Occur!" The Volstead Act had become law and the nation went dry.

Or more accurately, the nation's rivers of booze went underground and gave rise to a new industry: bootlegging. Almost overnight a vast criminal enterprise sprang up across the nation and gangsters became rich and powerful running whiskey and operating secret, password-protected bars. None became more powerful than the New York born Alphonse Capone.

Capone made his name in Chicago as the head of the vaguely named "Chicago Outfit," even though his business card referred to him as a used furniture dealer. In truth he was an accomplished manager of a network of bootleggers. Occasionally, the "heat" in Chicago would cause him to take refuge in the comfort of the Julien Inn in Dubuque, Iowa, where he frequently availed himself of a favorite whiskey, Templeton Rye.

The tiny town of Templeton is located in northwest Iowa, about an hour-and-half drive from Des Moines in Carroll County. The story goes that, just before Prohibition, a traveler wandered through town and had heard that there may be some libations to be had. Stopping at the first house he came to, he inquired where it might be found. The kindly woman pointed to a yellow house down the street. "That house," she explained, "is the only house that doesn't sell Templeton Rye." That house was the Rectory.

When Prohibition took hold, and revenue agents or "revenuers" seemed to be everywhere, such openness and generosity vanished, although Templeton Rye did not. No one knows how many households continued to "cook whiskey," and only a select few will admit it even to this day, so strict were each family's secrecies, and so feared were the revenuers.

One family though, the descendents of Alphonse and Frances Kerkhoff, proudly proclaim the prowess of the family's prohibition-era recipe, and now Iowan's can enjoy it legally for the first time. Templeton Rye is now a licensed distilled spirit made only in Templeton and available only in Iowa.

Rye whiskey differs from its cousins, bourbon and scotch in numbers of ways, most notable that it must, by law, contain a minimum of 51% rye grain. Rye's contribution to the flavor of a whiskey is a spiciness, and it adds a sort of fruity dryness and a warmth to the finish, according to the late Michael Jackson, author of *Whiskey: The Definitive World Guide*. "What the rye grain gives to bread, it also imparts to whiskey," he writes. "Rye whiskey has that same hint of bitterness. It is reminiscent of bittersweet fruit—perhaps a hint of apricot—spicy, a little oily, almost peppermint."

While Jackson tells us of Rye's origins in colonial Pennsylvania and Maryland, it is Templeton's bootlegging history that the Kerkhoff's son Meryl, grandson (and master distiller) Keith, and great-grandson Kody hope will attract the attention of Iowa's (and some day the nation's) whiskey connoisseurs. They proudly flaunt the Capone connection and their family recipe's prohibition-era bona fides in all the marketing. The revenuers caught Alphonse and Frances Kerkhoff three times back then, the third offense leading to prison time for Alphonse.

Some of the best stories are of the secret hiding places people would use to store, or in some cases distribute, the contraband whiskey. One story Meryl likes to tell was that his mother was told the jug was hidden behind the toilet tank, and if any strangers were to come in the yard, she should dump the contents down the stool right away, before even opening the door because it might be a revenuer. One day while Alphonse was out it happened, and Frances dutifully dumped the whole gallon of whiskey only to find that it was just a salesman in her yard.

All this makes for great marketing, but still, it is the supple, amazingly smooth flavor that results from Minnesota rye, distilled and triple-filtered, then aged in oak barrels from Missouri that really win the palates of whiskey enthusiasts around the country. Templeton Rye was very well received at April's "WhiskeyLive" event in New York City, where many patrons called it the best of the show. This summer, they plan to unveil a limited edition batch in honor of the town of Templeton's Quasquicentennial July 6 – 8.

The Kerkhoff's hope to be licensed to sell their Rye in Chicago by this fall, and around the country soon after, but for now legalities and a supply keep it exclusively in Iowa. Lucky us.

Traditional Rye Cocktails

Two famous cocktails are traditionally made with Rye, the Sazerac and the Manhattan.

Sazerac:

- 1 teaspoon Pernod or Herbsaint liqueur
- Ice cubes
- 1 teaspoon sugar, 1 sugar cube, or 1 teaspoon simple syrup
- 1 1/2 ounces rye whiskey
- 3 dashed Peychaud's Bitters
- 1 lemon peel twist

Put the Pernod or Herbsaint in a chilled old-fashioned glass and swirl to coat the bottom and sides completely.

Discard the excess.

In a cocktail shaker combine 4-5 ice cubes with the sugar, rye, and bitters. Shake and strain into the old-fashioned glass. Twist the lemon peel over the glass to extract oils, then drop in the twist and serve.

Manhattan:

- 1 1/4 ounces rye whiskey
- 1/2 ounces sweet vermouth
- 2-3 dashes Angostura bitters
- Maraschino cherry for garnish

In a mixing glass with ice, combine the rye, vermouth, and bitters. Stir and strain into a cocktail glass, garnished with the cherry.

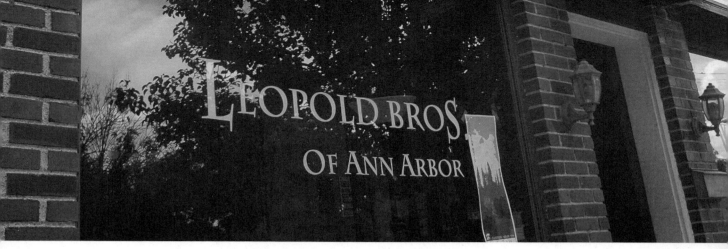

Sustainability as Business Model
The Leopold Brothers Brewery.

ANN ARBOR, MI – Imagine for a moment what the bar closest to the University of Michigan's 107,501-seat football stadium must be like. Most likely, you are picturing multiple plasma-screen televisions drowned out by very loud music and accented by neon beer signs and maize-and-blue pennants. You would also expect Saturday nights with buxom "Bud Girls," "light" beer, and crazed Wolverine fans.

You would be right about one thing: Wolverines fans do indeed like the Leopold Bros. Brewery on South Main Street, just a few blocks north of Michigan's mammoth football stadium. What you would not find there, though, are any of the trappings of a sports bar. Instead, Scott and Todd Leopold have created the world's first, and only, as far as I've been able to discern, environmentally sustainable brewery and distillery (though there is an all organic brewpub called Ukiah Brewing Company in Ukiah, CA). You might assume Scott and Todd to be a couple of tree-hugging hippies with a trust fund to play with, and you would be wrong again.

Descendants of the accomplished environmentalist Aldo Leopold (for whom the Leopold Center for Sustainable Agriculture at Iowa State University is named), Scott is an environmental engineer while brother Todd made his bones in small breweries in Germany. Their goal is to make great beer. Environmental sustainability is simply a means to that end. Scott says, "It's just a sound business model." Ironically, neither knew much about their famous ancestor's activism until the project was already well underway.

Walking in the front door, the first thing you would notice about the brewery is how open and airy the space is. The front room, the bar, is roughly fifteen hundred square feet of the 1927 Theo O. Aprill auto parts building. By removing the floor of the second level, Scott and Todd let in natural light through monitor windows in the roof, high above thick wooden crossbeams. Brewing only during daylight hours all but eliminates the need for electric light. The furniture, mostly picnic tables, is made entirely from reclaimed materials. Airflow is regulated by enormous "duct sox," fabric ducts which improve efficiency by even distribution of air. In place of televisions, there is a wide selection of popular board games.

A typical brewery produces ten glasses of wastewater for every bottle of beer it produces. The Leopolds reengineered the process to reduce that ratio to an industry best 1:1, and that one glass of water is reclaimed in an adjacent greenhouse, where they grow plants hydroponically.

You will find none of these facts on their labels or their advertising. It is mentioned here and there, a blurb in the menu, a sign on the door; but otherwise they barely mention, for example, that all their beers are organic. They don't need to. Their goal is "to quench the thirsts of today's beer drinkers without limiting the ability of future generations to do the same." Using all organic ingredients is just the logical means to that end. Putting "organic" on the label might compel one person to admire it, another to dismiss it, and both for the same (wrong) reason. Scott and Todd want their guests to judge the beer by the only measure that counts: flavor.

Flavor is the one thing that Leopold Bros. may have in excess. These are world-class beers, the kind you want to grip with a strong fist and savor each swallow as a bit of the head drizzles down your chin. They make a Pilsner that's much richer than the Americanized version. The "Schwarzbier" is, as the name implies, black beer, but smooth not bitter. The golden lager may be the closest to what commercial beer drinkers are used to in color, but in flavor it's all about two-row malt and flowery hops. Hefeweizen, sometimes called white or wheat beer, is a variety I never quite liked, but Leopold Bros. changed my mind about that. Munich malt gives color, and four different varieties of hops lend balance to the Red Lager. Each year around football season, the Oktoberfest brew rings in autumn with the beer's characteristic body and nutty Vienna malt.

These are aggressive beers, ranging in alcohol content from 4.2% to 6.7% by volume, with flavors meant for people who like beer to taste like much more than yellow carbonated water. This firm defense of quiet material pleasure demonstrates the importance of ecogastronomy. It is selfish and pointless to enjoy these things if we do not also preserve them, and by extension the means to produce them. Leopold Bros. Brewery is a guiding light.

Devotay Chocolate Mousse

Cooking with beer is sometimes a quandary for some people. When asked to develop a dessert that used beer, I came up with this around 1997 and have been making it ever since

Served in a wine glass at my restaurant, this dessert is often called sex in a glass by the wait staff. It is seductive, voluptuous and decadent, the way a chocolate dessert should be.

Besides being great on its own, it is also delicious frozen in a parfait or topped with brandy-soaked cherries.

> 1/2 pound semisweet chocolate, chopped (we use Scharffen Berger)
> 1 cup heavy cream, chilled
> 1/4 cup sugar
> 3 eggs, separated, room temperature
> 1/4 teaspoon cream of tartar
> 1/2 teaspoon vanilla extract
> 1/8 cup port wine
> 1/4 cup stout, room temperature

Melt the chocolate in a steel bowl over a double boiler. Be careful never to get water in the melted chocolate – this will cause the fats and solids to separate or "seize," and you'll have quite a mess on your hands. As the chocolate melts, whip the heavy cream and the sugar to a stiff peak. Getting any of the cream into the egg whites, or any of the whites into the cream, before they are both whipped to peaks will cause them not to whip up at all, so wash the mixing bowl and whip thoroughly between each step. Separately from the cream, whip the egg whites cream, of tartar and vanilla to stiff peaks. Then fold the whipped whites into the whipped cream.

Pour your melted chocolate into a mixer bowl. Using a paddle attachment, beating thoroughly after each addition, add yolks to the chocolate mixture one at a time, alternating with splashes of the port and stout until all are incorporated into the chocolate. This can be a little tricky, as the booze can make the chocolate seize just like the water can. Be sure to put one egg yolk in before any of the booze, and alternate between them. Scrape the sides of the bowl frequently along the way for a smoother mix.

Slowly fold one fourth of the cream/white mixture into the chocolate. Then fold the chocolate mixture back into the whites and cream, folding gently until no cream or lumps are visible. Portion into their serving cups, and chill thoroughly before serving.

Makes 6-8 dessert portions.

By the Shores of Gitche Gumee

Steve Dahl, Russ Kendall, and the Lake Superior Smoked Fish Tradition.

> *Forth upon the Gitche Gumee,*
> *On the shining Big-Sea-Water,*
> *With his fishing-line of cedar,*
> *Of the twisted bark of cedar,*
> *Forth to catch the sturgeon Nahma,*
> *Mishe-Nahma, King of Fishes,*
> *In his birch canoe exulting*
> *All alone went Hiawatha.*
> —HW Longfellow, Song of Hiawatha

KNIFE RIVER, MN – Steve Dahl is an endangered species.

Dahl is one of only twenty-five commercial fishermen left on the Minnesota side of Lake Superior. Almost every day, unless the lake is frozen, he will launch his eighteen-foot steel boat and head out to haul up his gill nets. Sometimes his dogs, a pair of handsome white Siberians, keep him company. It's very hard work, hoisting these nets full of herring from a depth of between twenty-four and forty-eight feet, but he was meant for this work. You can see his Viking ancestors in his eyes and in his hands.

The only thing Steve would change, if he could, would be that he'd fish for lake trout too. Only the sport fishers can take those, though. In the 1960s an invasive fish called the sea lamprey decimated the Lake Superior lake trout. In the decades since, careful regulation has brought the lamprey under control and reinvigorated the stocks of lake trout. So much so that the sport fishers took more than 15,000 of them in 2003, but still Dahl and his fellow professionals are not allowed.

Still he does fairly well selling his herring to restaurants and markets from Duluth northward. A true renaissance man, Dahl built his own smoker for fish. Constructed of stone, it stands a few yards from the Norwegian-style log home he built himself, by hand, about a mile from the shore. There he lives with his wife, Georgeann Hunter. An accomplished harpist, she has recorded two solo CDs and five more with the Celtic group Willowgreen. Many of her harps were handmade by Dahl.

A talented woodworker, he combined his interest in his wife's harps with his own growing interest in his heritage. This led him to Gjøvik, Norway, to learn the craft of making their ancient traditional instrument, the langeleik. Today he sells his handcrafted versions of this ancestor of the dulcimer to enthusiasts all over the world.

Still, his main livelihood is on the Big Lake, pulling up the herring that he sells to places like Russ Kendall's Smoked Fish in nearby Knife River. The late Russ Kendall's family-run operation has been selling smoked local fish to tourists and residents for nearly one hundred years. A quirky place, they sell all that smoked fish from a deli case in one room, which is attached to a bar, pool hall, and antique showroom in another. The brick smokers, coal black from decades of use, are at the back of the building.

At Kendall's you can taste the herring that Dahl so painstakingly hauls up each morning, smoked over hardwoods usually that very same day. You can also sample their delicious lake trout, but they didn't get that from Steve - they got that from Wisconsin or Ontario, where limited commercial fishing of lake trout is allowed.

Different fish swim in different depths of water, so people like Steve, in their longboats, could place their nets on the bottom and not affect the stocks of other gamefish, like steelhead and salmon that draw so many sport fishers to the area every year. A couple hundred lake trout would mean a big boost to Steve's bottom line, supplying the local restaurants through the peak tourist season – thereby supporting those restaurants, too.

Still, the Minnesota Department of Natural Resources remains cautious, trying to balance the interests of Dahl and his fellow professionals with those of the lake trout and the political implications of the tourist trade in the area. Dahl feels that the professionals would be very effective stewards. Who, he reasons, would have a greater stake in protecting the stocks than those whose livelihoods depend on them?

Regardless of how the battle turns out, one taste of the sugared lake trout from Russ Kendall's will convince anyone that there needs to be a lot more trout, and a lot more of it caught, by the shores of Gitche Gumee.

Smoked Lake Trout Mousse

If you can get Russ Kendall's Sugared Lake trout, that's the thing to use for this dish, or smoke your own. In a pinch, almost any boneless smoked fish will work with this recipe. If it's a particularly oily fish, like smoked bluefish, you may want to adjust the amount of cream.

I've been making variations on this recipe in my restaurant and others for years and years, and serving it with simple whole-wheat crackers. I'm always amazed when someone asks for more crackers – I'd bet I could eat a whole serving on one.

> 1 pound smoked lake trout
> 1 tablespoon horseradish
> 1 1/2 cups heavy cream
> 1 lemon, juiced
> 1 pinch white pepper

In a food processor, chop the trout fine, to the consistency of cornmeal. Remove to a large bowl, and fold in remaining ingredients. Chill and serve with bread or crackers.

Serves about 8 people as an appetizer, and the recipe scales well. Halve or double it at your leisure; just watch the consistency by adding the cream gradually.

Got Organic Milk?

Traders Point Creamery and the Practical Use of Biodynamics.

ZIONSVILLE, IN – About 25 minutes from downtown Indianapolis, just a stone's throw from the I-465's outer belt, lays land so pristine you would think you had used a time machine to get there rather than a car. These rolling pastures and lush meadows are home to about 120 head of Brown Swiss cows, several dozen laying hens, countless honeybees, all a part of Trader's Point Creamery.

What sets this dairy apart from others is their adherence to a system of agriculture called Biodynamics. Predating the organic farming movement by at least 20 years, Biodynamics is the brainchild of Rudolf Steiner, whose stunning body of work prompted biographer Stewart Easton to write in *Rudolf Steiner: Herald of A New Epoch*:

> "If Steiner had been nothing but a philosopher, or theologian, or educator, or authority on Goethe, or agricultural expert, or architect, or knowledgeable in medicinal plants, or dramatist, or gifted artistic innovator, inventor of eurhythmy, an age that respects specialization would have reserved a special niche for him. But Steiner was all these things at the same time."

That list does not even mention Biodynamics, the field for which Steiner is best remembered today. The idea is to treat the earth as a living thing that must be cared for and nurtured to keep it healthy. The presupposition is that the earth is sick, and the evidence for earth's illness is in the trees, the plants, the water, the soil, and even the weather. Symptoms like deforestation, global warming, soil erosion and farm chemical pollution all demonstrate this illness.

Steiner suggested that the farm is the basic unit of agriculture, and that a farm could be entirely self-sustaining, with just enough animals to provide manure for fertile soil, and that these animals would, in turn, be fed by the very products that fertile soil produced. If the farm is the basic unit of agriculture, then the soil is the basic unit of the farm.

Soil is seen as a living entity within the constructs of Biodynamics. Its millions of microscopic organisms live in symbiosis with the plants that take root in it, providing nutrition for the plants and receiving it in return. When this cycle is interrupted, as with chemical fertilizers, the soils becomes ill and eventually dies.

The study of Biodynamics can (and has) filled volumes, but what does all this have to do with a dairy in Indiana?

Simple. Healthy soil makes healthy grass. Healthy grass means healthy cows. All of the cows at Trader's Point live on the grassy pastures that surround the dairy itself, and are brought in only for milking and in case of bad weather. The result is sweet, satisfying, nutritious dairy products that the big industrial dairies can't even approach.

One of the big issues in the dairy world today is a something called rBGH, or Recombinant Bovine Growth Hormone. Its chemical name is Bovine Somatotropin (BST). While a cow's pituitary gland naturally produces bovine growth hormone, just like yours naturally produces human growth hormone, the health effects of supplementing the naturally occurring hormone with the laboratory-made (recombinant) hormone are unknown.

The dairy equivalent of steroids in baseball, rBGH is the industry's attempt to obtain higher yields and faster results through the use of drugs – something that used to be called "better living through chemistry." The hormone can increase milk production in treated dairy cattle by as much as 25%, so that farmers can literally "milk" more profits from each cow. Ironically, this abundance causes prices to drop, exacerbating the problems of small farms.

Originally there were several companies vying to supply dairy farmers worldwide to with rBGH, but they eventually dropped out of the running, leaving agribusiness giant Monsanto the sole manufacturer of BST. They call it Posilac®. Each package of Posilac® carries these warnings:

"Use of Posilac® has been associated with increases in cystic ovaries and disorders of the uterus during the treatment period. Cows injected with Posilac® may have small decreases in gestation length and birth weight of calves and may have increased twinning rates. Also the incidence of retained placenta may be higher following subsequent calving….

"Cows injected with Posilac® are at an increased risk of clinical mastitis. The number of cows affected with clinical mastitis and the number of cases per cow may increase. In addition, the risk of sub-clinical mastitis (milk not visibly abnormal) is increased. In some herds, use of Posilac® has been associated with increases in somatic cell counts….

"Use of Posilac is associated with increased frequency of use of medication in cows for mastitis and other health problems.

"Cows injected with Posilac® may experience periods of increased body temperature unrelated to illness…Use of Posilac® may result in an increase in digestive disorders such as indigestion and diarrhea…

"Studies indicated that cows injected with Posilac® had increased numbers of enlarged hocks and lesions… and second lactation calves had more disorders of the foot region however results of these studies did not indicate that use of Posilac® increased lameness."

Sounds pretty lame to me.

At any rate, many of these side effects lead to the increased use of antibiotics to fight off the infections in the lesions and on the teats and udders of the cows. According to the Cancer Prevention Coalition (www.PreventCancer.com), use of rBGH also leads to increased levels of something called "Insulin-like Growth Factor 1" (IGF-1) in the milk. Their website states "IGF-1 is a normal growth factor. Excess levels have been increasingly linked by modern research to human cancer development and growth."

Of course, since Monsanto's political connections are very strong, you will find no laws requiring that milk carry labels or warnings about the use of rBGH in the dairy cows that produced the milk. You will however find that Monsanto is working hard to stop those who do not use their product, like Trader's Point, from being allowed to say so on their labels. In addition, Canada and the European Union have banned importation of US milk precisely because of the use of rBGH.

Because they avoid the use of such noxious chemicals, Trader's Point produces some of the sweetest soul-nourishing milk you can imagine. They call it "creamline" because it is not homogenized, but it is pasteurized, which saves them the challenges faced by their fellow Hoosiers at the Apple Family Farm. In addition to the creamline milk, they also produce whole milk yogurt, honey, milk soap, ice cream, grass-fed beef and pasture-raised eggs.

Taking things a step further, Trader's Point now hosts a year-round all-organic farmers market, and in the summer they serve an all-organic meal to the market patrons right there on Trader's Point's scenic grounds

It takes very little self-awareness to realize that everything we put in our bodies has an effect on our bodies, and the next, even simpler logical conclusion is the fewer things that are artificial, the better.

Simple Homemade Ricotta Cheese

A great way to use milk when you have a little too much is to make your own cheese. The easiest to make is ricotta, and it is wonderful in lasagnas, raviolis, and pizza or simply spread on a piece of toast.

> 8 cups whole raw milk (pasteurized will work too)
> 1 cup buttermilk
> Salt and white pepper to taste
> Chopped fresh herbs such as basil, rosemary or chives (optional)

In a large soup pot, combine the milk and buttermilk. Place over medium heat with a thermometer so you can monitor the temperature as it rises. Do not stir.

The moment the mixture reaches 180°f, remove it from the heat and let stand for one hour.

Meanwhile, line a large strainer with cheesecloth, and be sure to have some excess hanging over the edge of the strainer. After the milk mixture has stood for an hour, and solids have begun to form, pour it into the lined strainer. If you wish to add some herbs, fold them in at this point.

Carefully gather the corners of the cheesecloth together to form a pouch. Tie them together with string and tie the string to the faucet of your sink (keep the cats away!). It will drip overnight, and in the morning, you'll have fresh ricotta cheese. Add salt and pepper, as little or as much as desired, then store refrigerated for up to one week.

Makes about 1 ½ quarts.

Tradition Meets Technology:

Herb and Kathy Eckhouse's La Quercia Prosciutto Americano.

NORWALK, IA – Four years in Parma, Italy, can teach you many things. One thing it is sure to teach is an appreciation of fine artisanal hams. After living in Parma for that time, learning all they could about artisanal prosciutto, Herb and Kathy Eckhouse returned to Iowa with the belief that the techniques had they learned in Italy could be well applied to the fabulous pork being raised in the Heartland.

Sometimes you don't know just how right you can be.

"La Quercia" means "the oak," and it is the symbol of the region of Parma, a reference to the majestic oaks whose acorns once fed the pigs of Parma. It is also Iowa's state tree – sufficient serendipity to name an Iowa-based prosciutto company after it.

La Quercia began in 2000. The Eckhouses' dream was to make a prosciutto of their own, but in the meantime, they began by importing the prosciutto of one of the best prosciutto makers in Parma. This helped them learn some of the ropes, build a distribution network, and work on the financing of their new plant in Norwalk, just south of Des Moines.

They also began experimenting with homemade hams of their own. Using techniques they had learned in Parma and making adjustments for the meat that was raised close to home, they closed in on the perfect combination of meat, salt, air, and time (the only ingredients in good prosciutto).

Making prosciutto is a slow process. It is not, as some major American cold-cut producers would have us believe, simply adding extra salt and pressing a cheap traditional American ham. There are no nitrates or nitrites to preserve it. The methods used in Parma, and now in Norwalk, have been refined by centuries of necessity. Refrigeration is a new process. For most of human existence we have had to preserve our meat through a myriad of curing, drying, and smoking techniques. The cultures around the Mediterranean were the best at it; from the cured Italian fatback known as *lardo* to the Spanish *bacalao*, or salt cod, there are thousands of them, and prosciutto could well be considered the king.

The process begins with the carefully trimmed ham, or hind leg, of the pig and echoes the seasonal cycle (winter, spring, and summer) followed for generations. It is salted and allowed to rest on one side in a cool place. After weeks in the cold (winter), the salt is rinsed off and the ham is hung to dry and develop its flavor in very specific climatic conditions for months.

You'll notice that a lot was left out of that process. Trimmed how? What kind of salt? Cured for how long? What temperatures? What specific climatic conditions? Well, if you can get that kind of information out of a prosciutto maker, then you are surprisingly more persuasive than I. Techniques are zealously guarded from family to family.

I can tell you a couple of the differences between the Prosciutto di Parma and those of San Danielle and Tuscany. In San Danielle, they press the ham under a weight to extract more liquid. This leads to an exceedingly sweet ham. In Tuscany, there is extra salt in the curing of the prosciutto, which I have always thought of as a compensation for the lack of salt in their bread.

The Eckhouses took what they had learned in Italy and combined it with some modern sanitation and refrigeration techniques. Herb would not tell me the precise times and temperatures, but I can tell you that the equipment used to accomplish his aims is state-of-the-art.

La Quercia's "green label" organic prosciutto made its world premiere in September 2005 at the Slow Food Iowa Harvest Dinner, a part of the Field to Family local food celebration held in Iowa City each year. Besides serving the ham naturale, simply sliced paper thin, Guest Chef Odessa Piper created 3 dishes featuring the marvelous new delicacy. First it was served in Puff Pastry with Sage and Northern Prairie "Parmesan" Goat Cheese (from Woodward, Iowa). Next she served it fried atop a chilled melon bisque, and finally, as part of a prosciutto-walnut compound butter on a pan-roasted Wholesome Harvest chicken breast.

Part of the beauty of prosciutto is that like the slow ideals themselves, it can appeal to nearly everyone, across any taste or socio-economic scale. Contrary to common misconception, prosciutto is not fancy food, and these ideals are not about food snobbery. Prosciutto is peasant food, a way to preserve and make delicious the otherwise lesser cuts of pork (because the chops and loins went to the nobles).

Herb and Kathy have transported this classic fare from its origins in the Italian countryside to the Heartland prairie where it has found a new home and new fans among America's modern farmers. This in turn provides a new market for the sustainable pork producers who supply La Quercia, and a local source for an imported delicacy.

Pasta Rolls with Prosciutto Americano

Kathy writes:

"Is there a story behind this recipe? It is a mélange of recipes from a variety of places, heavily influenced by 4 years in Parma, Italy. The ricotta/spinach filling is very similar to the filling for *tortelli di erbetta*, a regional specialty made with Swiss chard. I substituted spinach because Swiss chard is rarely available. Herb and I have made this recipe several times and people love it. It is best served the day it's made, but we have frozen small dishes of it successfully. I wouldn't care to take it on by myself, but it is a fun rainy day project!

For the Plain Pasta:
1 extra-large egg
I pinch salt
3/4 cup white, unbleached flour
For the Spinach Pasta
1 extra-large egg
1 pinch salt
1 cup white, unbleached flour
1 egg-sized lump of cooked, finely chopped spinach, squeeze out as
    much moisture as possible

For the Filling
1 cup or more homemade ricotta (see page 61)
1 or 2 eggs
1 cup Parmigiano Reggiano, finely grated
Salt and pepper to taste
For the White Sauce:
2 cups milk
4 tablespoons unsalted butter
3 tablespoons flour
½ teaspoon salt
For assembly
18-20 paper thin slices of Prosciutto
1 cups marinara sauce
Fresh grated Parmigiano Reggiano to taste

To make the plain pasta, make a mound of flour in a large bowl. Add salt. Form a well in the middle and crack the egg into it. Using a fork, gradually incorporate the flour with the egg, then use your hands to knead into smooth, elastic dough. Allow it to rest, covered tightly, for ½ hour before rolling.

Repeat this process for the spinach pasta, incorporating the spinach into the flour before adding the egg.

Roll pasta out thin and cut into 5" equilateral triangles (about 18). Cook briefly (about 2 minutes for al dente) in boiling, salted water and place on a clean, slightly dampened dish towel. Cover lightly and make filling.

To make the filling, mix the ricotta, Parmigiano, eggs, salt and pepper thoroughly and refrigerate

To make the white sauce, heat milk in a saucepan to scalding point. Melt butter in a separate saucepan. Make a roux by adding the flour, stirring constantly with a whisk. Cook over medium heat for about five minutes over medium heat, stirring frequently, and then add milk very slowly.

Add salt and cook stirring over low heat until desired thickness (like heavy cream).

Have plain pureed marinara sauce ready. Kathy says, " A very delicious summer sauce can be prepared by lightly cooking some garden ripe tomatoes (preferably a low moisture variety, passing them through the medium mesh of a food mill, and then reducing them to the desired thickness over moderate heat and salting to taste. Don't over-salt." Alternately, use a pureed version of the Devotay marinara recipe in this book.

Place a thin slice of La Quercia prosciutto on each pasta triangle. Place about three tablespoons of filling formed into a rough log on top of the prosciutto. Roll up from base to point of triangle.

Place a thin layer of white sauce on the bottom of an ovenproof baking dish. Place the pasta rolls in the dish. Spoon white sauce between triangles and lightly on top. Spoon a ring of tomato sauce around the outer edge of the dish. Put more white sauce in middle and top with grated Parmigiano Reggiano. Do not over sauce.

Bake at 350 to 400 degrees for 15 minutes. The dish should be thoroughly hot and very slightly golden on top. Do not overheat or over brown. This dish is delicate, savory, and luscious and should be treated tenderly.

Makes about 18 rolls, and serves 6 as an entree

A Different Central Coast:

The Wines of Tabor Hill.

BUCHANAN, MI – So, you're hosting a dinner party, and you want to have a little fun, hence you organize a quick blind taste test. You pour a white wine for everyone from a bottle wrapped with foil or brown paper, and ask your guests to take a shot at naming the grape and the origin.

Your friends find the wine delicious, dry with a pleasant green apple fruit, nice acid balance and structure. All are agreed that it makes an excellent choice for the hot summer evening.

"Sauvignon Blanc from New Zealand!" one quickly and confidently shouts. "No," says another, "California Chardonnay – no oak." Perhaps someone will offer a more adventurous guess, such as Pinot Blanc or Viognier.

It worked; you've stumped them all. Sure, chardonnay was close. Your secret wine was made from a new hybrid cross of French Chardonnay and American Seval Blanc now known as Chardonel, but they never would have got that. You were even more confident that they would miss the appellation, too.

"No way!" they seem to shout in unison, "Michigan? Harrumph, harrumph."

That's right. Michigan. Meet Tabor Hill, the most successful winery in the Wolverine State. Nestled on seventy acres of rolling vineyards just a short drive from the shores of Lake Michigan, Tabor Hill has been making wine since 1968 (that's longer than more than half of the wineries in California). This is not the sort of winery that makes syrupy sweet wines from fruits like strawberries and cherries, for the amusement of the RV tourists who cruise the Great Lakes every summer. Nor is it a struggling little operation that makes wine from grapes you never heard of.

Tabor Hill produces 100,000 gallons of wine every year, and a vast majority of the varieties are *Vitis vinifera*, the classic wine grapes such as Pinot Noir, Chardonnay, Merlot and

Cabernet Sauvignon. Most impressive, though, is their Chardonel. The vine was created in a joint venture between Tabor Hill and Michigan State and Cornell Universities to develop a variety of chardonnay that could withstand the harsh winters of the Great Lakes region. They succeeded admirably, through old-fashioned botany and careful selection rather than messing around with some sort of genetically modified frankenwine.

Situated on the sandy clay soil of southwest Michigan, straight across the lake from Chicago, Tabor Hill is protected from the late spring freezes by hills that were formed by the same glaciers that made the Great Lakes. Throughout the area, farms grow not just vines, but a wide variety of crops, notably berries and apples. These, in turn, can be picked up at the farm stands that seem to proliferate throughout the area.

Tabor Hill has a restaurant on site managed by Paul Landeck. Paul, as it happens, is also the leader of Slow Food Michiana – a convivium that straddles the state's southern border to include South Bend, Indiana. Each gathering conducted by Slow Food Michiana begins with the same simple toast "To the simple pleasures of Slow Food, good friends, and the joy they bring us tonight." One of those gatherings might even be at the Tabor Hill vineyard restaurant, allowing one to enjoy local cherries and other berries from the region. Wine maker Mike Merchant works with Paul and the kitchen staff to match Tabor Hill's wines with the meals served. Besides the aforementioned Chardonel, they offer a wide range of dry, semi-sweet and sweet wines to suit any palate and any plate.

Peach Chardonnay Vinaigrette

Guests at the Tabor Hill restaurant run by Paul Landeck love this unique salad dressing, made with vinegar and grapeseed oil produced right there at the winery.

I've changed it just a bit, using less sugar than was originally called for, but that's a matter of taste – you should increase or decrease that according to your own palate.

> 2 cups fresh peaches
> ½ cup Tabor Hill Chardonnay vinegar
> ½ teaspoon salt
> ¼ teaspoon ground pink peppercorns
> ¾ cup sugar
> ¼ teaspoon fresh orange zest
> Pinch of cayenne pepper
> 1 ½ cups Tabor Hill grapeseed oil

Puree the peaches until smooth. Pour into a large bowl, then whisk in the vinegar and the rest of the ingredients except the oil.

In a slow, steady stream, pour the oil into the peach mixture while whisking constantly. You can use a food processor here; however the blades move so fast that they actually create heat that can make the oil taste bitter. Doing it by hand takes only a moment longer.

When all the oil is incorporated, taste for salt and sugar, adjust accordingly, then refrigerate. It will keep about 2 weeks in refrigeration. Makes about 4 cups.

In the Shadow of a Behemoth

The Schlafly Taproom and Bottleworks.

St. Louis, MO – In 1857, when Adolphus Busch arrived in St. Louis, Missouri, there were forty breweries in the city. By 1861, he had met and married the daughter of the owner of the twenty-ninth largest brewery in St. Louis. Her name was Lilly, and her father was Eberhardt Anheuser. Three years later Busch was working for his father-in-law at E. Anheuser and Co. By 1875 he was the secretary/treasurer. When Mr. Anheuser died in 1880, Busch was named president. In 1883, he acquired the rights to bottle and sell Budweiser, and the "King of Beers" was born.

Adolphus did not survive to see passage of the Volstead Act, the law that implemented Prohibition and effectively annihilated brewing in St. Louis and the rest of the country. But he had built a strong and savvy company, and Anheuser-Busch (AB) survived by manufacturing nonalcoholic "near beer," soda, and yeast. When Repeal was finally enacted in 1933, it was the new Budweiser Clydesdales that delivered beer to Washington, D.C. At this point, there were five surviving breweries in the United States, and AB owned two of them.

More than seventy years later, AB is, by far, the largest American brewer, selling 136.1 million barrels of beer worldwide and grossing more than $17 billion in 2004. Garrett Oliver, Brewmaster of the Brooklyn Brewery and a Slow Food International Councilor, describes what Anheuser-Busch does as miraculous. "When you combine yeast with grain and water," Oliver says, "it tries very hard to create flavor. Budweiser's ability to retard that tendency, to tame the flavor to suit the broadest number of palates, and to do so on a consistent basis is nothing short of amazing."

In 1980, there were only forty-four breweries in the US, all of them making approximately the same beer, an adjunct light lager that they had carefully groomed the marketplace to prefer. Then something magical happened. People began to wonder what it would be like if their beer actually tasted different from their water. By 2001, 1,458 "craft" breweries were producing 6.23 million barrels a year. A drop in the beer barrel compared to AB's 136 million, but it was enough for them to take notice. They began to buy shares in microbreweries like Redhook, and marketed new brands of there own made to look like craft-brewed beers while simultaneously dumbing-down the beers at the newly acquired "craft" brewers. Their practice of making flavorless, character-devoid beers while relentlessly advertising their great taste in a perverse, Orwellian manner would continue unabated.

Meanwhile, in AB's own backyard, a quiet revolution was fomenting (or should I say, fermenting?)

The Schlafly Tap Room was opened by founder and president Tom Schlafly in 1991 and was Missouri's first brewpub. He hired a local brewing authority and author of several books on homebrewing named Dave Miller as the brewmaster, and an assistant named Stephen Hale. In 2003, they opened a second enterprise, Bottleworks, the first new bottling brewery in St. Louis since the late 1930s. Besides brewing some thirty-six different types of beer (six year round and the rest seasonally), they operate both locations with entirely separate menus with locally raised ingredients where feasible including bread from Companion Bakery over on Gustine Avenue.

Once a month, Bottleworks hosts Slowednesday, an opportunity to get to know your food, its origins, and the local farmers who produce it. They sacrificed half an acre of their parking lot to install an organic community garden, and they host a Farmers' Market in another part of that lot every Wednesday throughout the season.

Now Chief Brewer, Stephen Hale, lives right in the shadow of AB's enormous brewery, in the historic old St. Louis neighborhood called Soulard. Originally built as a sort of company town for the brewery workers, it has since become a quaint tree-lined neighborhood of local pubs and renovated brownstones, and all those local pubs are pouring Schlafly beer. No word on whether Eberhardt or Adolphus would have appreciated the irony.

St. Louis was once an undisputed titan of the brewing world, but the lingering effects of Prohibition and the uncanny marketing abilities of Anheuser-Busch have swept away storied old names like Falstaff, Carling Black Label and Highland Bohemian. But artisans like Stephen Hale at Schlafly Brewing are working to create a better beer culture for all of St. Louis to enjoy.

Sticky Toffee Pudding

Stephen Hale, The Schlafly Bottleworks and Taproom, St. Louis, MO

Of this sinful dessert, Schlafly Brewmaster Stephen Hale had this to say: "The STP is the only item on the menus of both locations. Although the emphasis of the Bottleworks is heavy on local, organic, fresh, Slow food, the STP is the eternal item, perhaps like fish and fries at the Tap Room. The reason I prefer it is that when it is ordered for a table, it's very easy to share this sinful dessert with four people, lingering at a snail's pace with our Oatmeal Stout (or coffee); there are plenty of diners who can consume one alone, but sharing it is what it's all about.

"Although the ingredients don't necessarily emphasize local (fresh whipped cream, and eggs, from a nearby farm, there we go!), the pace of consumption fits the category better than most things. We might have a particular menu item at the Bottleworks with a lot of local ingredients, but that will change over time; the STP is as permanent as it gets, after fourteen years we're pretty sure of this! Sara and I even had it made up in New Hampshire for our rehearsal dinner six years ago, so there's an endorsement."

This is a large recipe, best made for a party. However it does scale well if you like – simply cut every measurement in half and bake in a smaller pan.

For the Pudding:
1 pound pitted dates, chopped fine
2 cups hot water
2 teaspoons baking soda
5 ounces butter, unsalted
1 pound sugar
2 teaspoons vanilla extract
5 large eggs
1 pound white, unbleached flour
2 teaspoon baking powder
1 pinch salt

Preheat the oven to 350°

Grease 1 9" x 13" pan (or equivalent) with butter and coat lightly with flour, shake out excess flour. In conventional restaurant parlance, a stainless steel baking pan this size is referred to as a "hotel pan," and is usually 2 inches deep unless otherwise noted. If you scale the recipe in half, obviously use a smaller pan.

Combine dates with hot water in a 3-quart saucepan and bring to a boil. Remove the pan from heat and add the baking soda. Set aside to cool.

In a mixing bowl cream butter, sugar and vanilla on high speed for 3 minutes.

With mixer on low speed, add eggs one at a time until fully incorporated. Add flour, baking powder, and salt.

When fully mixed fold in the dates and their liquid.

Place batter into greased pan and bake in preheated oven until a skewer inserted comes out clean (30-45 minutes).

Cool on a baking rack before removing from the pan.

For the Caramel:

1 pound dark brown sugar
1 pound butter
1 teaspoon vanilla extract
1 cup heavy cream

Stir together first three ingredients on low heat until blended and brown sugar has melted.

Whisk heavy cream into the mixture.

To Serve:

Spoon warm caramel sauce over 1 serving portion of Sticky Toffee Pudding.

Top with a dollop of freshly whipped cream and a mint sprig, if you like.

Serves 24

RESTAURANTS AND MARKETS

"I'm a cook. It's a simple, direct profession. I prepare a dish, I send it out to the
guest, I see the results immediately. On a busy Saturday night, when the juices are really
flowing, I get to score a touchdown a minute. I can think of no other profession that is
more convivial or more rewarding."
—Chef Charlie Palmer, Great American Food

High-Flying Vegan Cuisine

Dragonfly Neo-V.

COLUMBUS, OH – I am not a vegan. I am not even a vegetarian. In fact, I have been caught once or twice poking fun at the practitioners from my omnivore's perch. I have since repented for that, and Dragonfly Neo-V is part of the reason.

Located between Columbus' Short North neighborhood and the campus of Ohio State University, Dragonfly is the brainchild of Magdiale Wolmark and Cristin Austin. Beginning in 2000, together they have built a restaurant that qualifies as one of the best (vegan or not) in this underrated restaurant town, and perhaps the best vegan restaurant in the country. The cuisine is strictly vegan, meaning no animal proteins or by-products of any kind (not even honey, I was surprised to learn), and strictly organic. They buy their produce from local area farms as much as possible, and have built a network of like-minded farmers to provide a steady supply. Locals such as Kevin Eigel of Just This Farm, Tim Patrick of Toadhill Farms, and Chanda Williams of First Fruits all contribute to the menu.

With all the fantastic ingredients available locally to this hip spot in the trendy section of Columbus, it becomes easy to see how one could have a delicious (and filling) meal without the meat, which is why Dragonfly made *USA Today*'s list of "Ten Best Places to Eat with an Easy Conscience." With no meat on the menu, there is no controversy.

Many people in America will not eat veal because of the cruel and inhumane way the calves are raised on factory farms – they are crated in very small pens on grates, unable to move or see the sun, and are given many hormones and antibiotics so that the feed doesn't kill them before they are slaughtered. Then some of these same people turn around and eat industrially produced chicken from the big grocery stores or chain restaurants, blissfully unaware of the unspeakable (and very brief) lives the birds lead.

One answer, if one does choose to eat meat, is to look to the small, local farmer who uses sustainable husbandry methods, such as those advocated by the American Livestock Breeds Conservancy, the first American recipient of the prestigious Slow Food Award for Biodiversity. Another organization that works hard on this is the Animal Welfare Institute. AWI "works to halt these intensive farming practices and replace them with methods which are both humane and practical," says their website. "Animal factories put family farmers out of business, endanger public health and pollute our air and water. It all begins with cruelty to animals in the factory."

Magdiale and Cristin avoid the controversy entirely by serving nothing from the animal kingdom. And, by buying locally and adhering to strict organic standards, they keep many other controversial substances off the menu as well (such as chemical fertilizers and unfair labor practices). Still, ever the skeptic, when I first approached Dragonfly I assumed I would, at best, leave hungry. "It couldn't be filling, couldn't be satisfying, even if they do have ways of making it tasty," I reasoned. This qualifies as one of those moments when one is pleased to be wrong.

Naturally, Dragonfly's menu changes with the seasons, sometimes even more frequently. At dinner, you might enjoy a wild walnut and grilled shiitake ravioli with Villa Manodori balsamic vinegar and microgreens. Follow that with a salad of Malabar spinach with more grilled shiitakes, chili-pickled candy onions, black walnuts, and dried tomato-smoked tofu vinaigrette. Remember, this is a devout omnivore telling you: don't be afraid of tofu – it is very versatile and an excellent source of protein.

Then, as long as we're on a mushroom binge, you may want to try a portobello-leek tart with poached king oyster (that's a mushroom, not a shellfish), eggplant confit and a star anise sauce.

Alternately, you may wish to enjoy a degustation of vegetables grown right there at the "chef's table," which is in the middle of their jardin potager, or kitchen garden, recently featured in Jennifer Bartley's book *Designing the New Kitchen Garden*.

If it were lunch you were after, you could sit on the patio and enjoy baby lettuce Niçoise, with black olives, peas, dried tomatoes, grilled smoked tofu, rosemary potatoes and aged balsamic vinaigrette. After that, try their Mediterranean pizza with tomato-olive sauce, marinated figs, grilled eggplant and white bean purée.

Now that you are sated, stop in and browse through their gallery and performance space next door. It too is dedicated to all things local, showcasing some of the best emerging talent on the vibrant Columbus arts scene. And don't forget to stop by their bakery and market, located right next door.

Dragonfly is a fine example of what "living slow" represents: The importance of the kitchen and the table as centers of our everyday lives; the spiritual satisfaction of shaking the hand that raised the food, or even digging in and raising it yourself.

"Backyard" Shiitake and Wild Foraged Black Walnut Tartare

Chef Magdiale grows his own shiitake mushrooms for this dish on a log in the back yard, and forages for the black walnuts that are prolific in central Ohio, thus the tartare's name.

This is a great dish to serve at your next party – everyone will be pleased with the combination of intense flavor and high nutritional value, something true of all the food at Dragonfly Neo-V.

Tamari is a form of soy sauce, originally a by-product of making miso. It is readily available at any Asian market, and now even many mainstream grocery stores. Home pickling is fairly easy, but if you must substitute with prepared ones, choose interesting flavors from a purveyor you trust.

¼ cup black walnuts, preferably wild
1 tablespoon fresh parsley, chopped
1 cup fresh shiitake mushrooms, rinsed, stemmed and chopped
½ teaspoon minced ginger
1 pinch salt
1 tablespoon tamari
1 dozen capers
1 teaspoon Walla Walla onion (or other very sweet onion), diced
3 homemade pickled vegetables such as okra, green cherry or "bread and butter"
1 teaspoon Dijon mustard
6 thin "croutes" or crostini, drizzled with sesame oil and grilled

In a food processor, pulse the walnuts until they are very finely ground, not quite a paste. Add parsley and Shiitakes and pulse 6 or 7 times until shiitakes are minced. Very important to stop here – as mushrooms lose water, the mixture will begin to bind. Add ginger and salt, and drizzle in tamari while pulsing 2 or 3 more times.

Remove mixture and form into a patty served with the crostini, and garnished with the capers, onion, pickle and mustard.

Serves 2-4 as an appetizer.

A Taste of Home

Forging a New Life on the Iron Range with the Foods of the Homeland.

CHISHOLM, MN – It was 1968 in Jan Gadzo's native Czechoslovakia. The rumblings of a new revolution, of throwing off the Soviet yoke, had become the hopeful season called the Prague Spring. Jan was quite active in supporting the reforms instituted by then First Secretary Alexander Dubcek that were dubbed "Socialism with a human face."

Such reforms were seen as a threat in the Kremlin, and following what was termed the Brezhnev Doctrine, the Soviets and the Warsaw Pact invaded Czechoslovakia on August 20 and 21, 1968. Gadzo knew that his life was in danger and that he had to get out. With the help of friends and family in America, he escaped probable execution and made it safely to New York in 1969.

Though happy to be safe and free, he missed his family and his homeland. Food was his one connection to his Slovak heritage. In 1979, when Jan and his wife Jean were driving across country from New Jersey to Minnesota, a stop to visit his aunt in Pittsburgh reintroduced a Slovak pastry called *potica* (pronounced "po-TEET-sa"). Jan's aunt gave the couple two of the traditional walnut rolls for the road, which were gone long before they made it to the Iron Range.

The Iron Range is a swath of land north of Duluth, so named for the iron mines that were dug throughout the region in the late 1800's. The mines attracted a large influx of immigrants, mostly middle Europeans and Finns, as well as the Welsh and the Cornish – the experienced miners of Great Britain. For more than a hundred years, these cultures and cuisines have melded there, and three resulting regional specialties have become solid traditions. It was this high concentration of fellow Slovaks that attracted Jan to staying in the Iron Range.

The Italian contribution to this triumvirate is *porketta*, a pork roast marinated in several spices for a couple of days before it is slow roasted and then either sliced for a dinner entree or pulled apart to serve on crusty rolls. The Cornish miners brought the *Pasty* (pronounced with a short "a" – PASS-tee), their version of the sort of meat-in-dough dumpling found in innumerable variation in almost every cuisine. Though most commonly filled with beef and potato, it actually could have almost any filling imaginable. There is a proverb that says that the devil himself would never dare cross the River Tamar into Cornwall for fear of winding up as filling in a Cornish pasty.

The Slovaks brought the potica, so the Gadzos felt right at home settling in the small mining town of Chisholm. Potica is a log-shaped pastry, filled most commonly with walnuts or poppy seeds, then baked and sliced. It is delicious with coffee (especially the very strong Slovak variety called kava) and is also tasty with thin slices of your favorite ham. Of course, since cuisine knows no boarders, potica is a dish claimed by many of the migrant cultures of the Iron Range. The Italians and Slovenians also claim it as their own, and their versions vary only slightly from one to the next.

This is not to say that the quality of them varies only slightly. To the contrary, like any pastry, a potica can be made well or poorly. It is the combination of the Old World recipe Jan received from his aunt in Pittsburgh, with the finest ingredients, twenty-plus years of experience, and a family's love that make the potica at Andrej's European Pastry in downtown Chisholm something special.

They opened a storefront location in 2001 which was named after the Gadzo's only son, Andrej. They supply restaurants and grocery stores in the area and sell over the internet around the world. On a good day, Gadzo can turn out 400 walnut or poppyseed poticas. They make a few other pastries, such as the popular kolaches, but a vast majority of what they do is the poticas. Today, sales are made by telephone, or internet orders.

Gadzo is understandably proud of his adopted homeland, his family here and the success of Andrej's. He is prouder still of his heritage, and is quick to point out the difference when I mention my own Czech heritage. "I am Slovak!" he insists, a reminder that unlike when he escaped tyranny there almost forty years ago, Slovakia is now its own free and sovereign nation.

Still, Gadzo prefers to stay in America, noting, "The only way I could stay with my family [back in Slovakia] is through the food."

Indeed as I have so often said, if you think about the very best times in your life, I'll bet that most of them were spent around a table with great food in front of you and the people you love all around. If the Slow Food movement is about anything, it is about making as many of those moments as possible. Jan is doing just that for his family and for many others around the country with his marvelous potica.

Walnut Potica

My powers of persuasion are not such that I could convince Jan Gadzo to part with that recipe he got from his aunt in Pittsburgh. However I've done a little baking in my time and after some research and a little experimenting, this is what I came up with.

Though this recipe is mighty good, I confess I did not quite reach Jan's mastery of it, but perhaps if I make hundreds every day for several years like he has, I'll begin to approach it.

This recipe makes two rolls, and is best served with vanilla ice cream and coffee.

For the Dough:
¾ cup sour cream
¾ cup scalded milk
¾ cup sugar
2 tablespoons yeast
6 ½ cups white, unbleached flour
1 cup butter, melted
8 egg yolks, beaten
2 teaspoons salt
1 egg (for glaze)

For the Filling:
1 cup scalded milk
1 ½ pounds toasted, ground walnuts
¼ pound butter
1 cup sugar
1 teaspoon vanilla extract
grated rind of 1 lemon
1 egg yolk

To maker the dough, mix the sour cream and scalded mixture thoroughly, and then pour milk over the sugar. Stir to dissolve the sugar. Allow to cool to about 95°, and then add the yeast.

Add 3 cups of the flour and beat well. This will make what's called a sponge. Cover and let rise in a warm place until sponge is full of bubbles, about 45 minutes.

Stir in the melted butter, egg yolks, salt and about 3 more cups of the flour – add more if needed to keep the dough from being to sticky. Knead until smooth. Cover and let rise again until doubled.

Preheat oven to 350°

Meanwhile, make the filling. Pour scalded milk over toasted, ground walnuts. Add butter, and stir to melt the butter. Add sugar, vanilla, lemon rind, and egg yolk. Allow to cool completely before using.

Divide the dough in half and turn out onto a floured board. Roll to a ¼"-thick rectangle. Spread half the filling on the rolled out dough and roll like a jelly roll. Place on a buttered sheetpan. Repeat for the other dough. Cover and them let rise again about 45 minutes, or until not quite doubled. Beat that last egg and brush the roll evenly all over the surface for a nice glaze.

Bake for 45 minutes to 1 hour or until browned and done. Makes 2 rolls.

Fifty Years of Family Food

Jasper's Restaurant and the Marco Polo Market.

KANSAS CITY, MO – Although it is probably best known for its barbecue, Kansas City does have a strong Italian-American heritage. Nowhere is this better represented than at the restaurant of third generation chef and owner Jasper J. Mirabile, Jr. Jasper's, a Kansas City institution, has been operated by Jasper Jr, his father and his father's father for more than fifty years. It has won accolades from nearly every quarter, including AAA four-diamond awards and Mobil four-star awards for twenty-five years. Legendary *New York Times* food writer Craig Claiborne called their veal limonata "a culinary dream" and included the recipe in one of his books. Jasper Jr. cooked at the prestigious James Beard House in 1995, and was invited back in 1996.

The tradition of the kitchen and the table as centers of our everyday lives has been in the Mirabiles' blood for generations. Nana and Papa, as Jasper Jr. affectionately knew them, immigrated to the United States from Sicily with the waves of immigrants following World War II. In 1954, Leonardo Mirabile (Papa) opened a little neighborhood restaurant and bar in Kansas City with his son, Jasper. Had you stopped in then, you may have enjoyed a Caesar salad, Fettucine Alfredo, and Scampi Livornese, all for seventy-nine cents.

Thirty years later, joined by the next generation of Mirabile boys, Leonard and Jasper Jr., they opened Marco Polo's Groceria. Six years later, a trattoria was added.

In 1999, Jasper's moved to its current location. Sadly, Jasper Sr., who started the relocation project, passed away before its completion. The new restaurant features increased seating, the grocery, trattoria and a new "Enoteca" (wine bar) with over four hundred wines to choose from. A spacious patio overlooks beautiful, rambling Indian Creek. Murals by Steve Murillo adorn the walls. The food, though, is the same traditional fare that has made Jasper's famous.

That is not to say it is stodgy. To the contrary, three generations worth of Mirabiles gather every Sunday in the family home to test new recipes. Authenticity is the key to their recipe development. Tradition means everything. A recipe in Jasper Jr.'s book, *The Jasper's Cookbook*, contains a recipe for Linguine with Clam Sauce, or Linguine alla Vongole, which calls for linguine, littleneck clams, olive oil, garlic, red pepper flakes, clam juice, white wine, and oregano. That's all. In a note on that page, Jasper cautions, "never put cream or cheese in this dish. In Italy it would be a sin."

Invigorating and proliferating regional, seasonal culinary traditions is important to the Mirabiles. It is not that there is anything inherently wrong with the new and the innovative in the world of cuisine, only that it is important to maintain a certain reverence for, and liveliness in, the traditions that have made food such an enjoyable part of our lives. They feel it would be sad if we were to lose the great foods of the world in some farcical, baby-with-the-bathwater scenario, all in the name of "the next new thing."

Writing the epilogue for *The Jasper's Cookbook*, Jasper sat on the deck of a ferry headed to Messina, Sicily from Reggio, Calabria. He noted that Nana and Papa had traveled these waters decades earlier, and had they not, he would not be who he is, where he is, earning accolades and cooking at the James Beard House.

It is his knowledge of what came before, and his reverence for it, that make his restaurant stand out.

Nana Jo's Grilled Lamb Chops

Jasper writes: "Every summer my Nana would prepare these delicious little chops on the grill. She would marinate the chops in balsamic and garlic and a little bit of red pepper. My three brothers and I would eat the chops faster than my dad could grill them!"

A note about your grill: Gas grills are adequate, and need to be heated roughly 1/2 hour in advance. Real wood always brings better flavor, though. I recommend using real wood charcoal, not briquettes. A charcoal fire needs about an hour to reach that white-ashed glow that's perfect to cook on.

> 2-3 lamb racks (about 3 pounds, or 12 chops)
> 1 lime, juiced
> 2 tablespoons brown sugar
> Salt to taste
> 5 tablespoons balsamic vinegar
> ½ cup extra virgin olive oil
> 4-5 sprigs fresh mint
> 2-3 cloves garlic, sliced paper thin
> ½ cup mint jelly

One day ahead: If your butcher hasn't already, cut the racks into chops, using a cleaver if necessary to separate the chine bone. Lay out the chops in a shallow casserole. Drizzle the juice from the lime on the chops.

Mix the brown sugar, salt, and balsamic vinegar with half of the olive oil. Chop 2 of the mint sprigs coarsely and add to this marinade. Pour the marinade over the chops, turning each to get them thoroughly coated. Marinate in the refrigerator overnight.

On the day of service: First thing in the morning, turn each chop once so that they marinate evenly.

Light the grill about an hour and a half before service. While the grill is warming up, mix the rest of the olive oil with the mint jelly and garlic.

Place the chops on the grill, being careful not to crowd your surface area. Grill them in batches if necessary. Baste each side with the mint sauce (Nana used a mint sprig to baste with). Cook approximately 5 minutes on each side, or to desired doneness. Serve immediately with remaining basting sauce for dipping. Serves 6.

Diversity as Dominant Paradigm

The Seed Savers Exchange.

DECORAH, IA – 30 years ago, Diane Ott Whealy was given a gift by her terminally ill grandfather. It was a gift handed down to him by his parents, who had brought it to their new world home of St. Lucas, Iowa, from Bavaria in the 1870s. Now he, in his last days, was continuing a tradition that goes back millennia - literally to the dawn of civilization – handing down the heritage that was Diane's birthright.

The gift was seeds. One was a variety of tomato known as the German Pink, and the other was a flower, Grandpa Ott's Morning Glory. A simple gift, to be sure, but one that would grow into something truly special just as surely as the seeds themselves held glorious bounty within their tiny shells. For Diane's grandfather had not simply planted a seed, he had planted an idea that would save the world.

Diane and her then-husband Kent created The Seed Savers Exchange (SSE) in 1975 from those two original seed varieties. Through a network of thousands of members around the world, Seed Savers, "is saving the world's diverse, but endangered, garden heritage for future generations by building a network of people committed to collecting, conserving and sharing heirloom seeds and plants," it says on their website, all "while educating people about the value of genetic and cultural diversity. Few gardeners comprehend the true scope of their garden heritage or how much is in immediate danger of being lost forever."

It has since grown into one of the world's largest guardians of heirloom seed diversity. Heirloom seeds are simply those that have been passed down through generations, like heirloom jewelry. They have not been genetically manipulated in any way. With the cooperation of more than eight thousand members worldwide, SSE is dedicated to saving these varieties because the world's botanical diversity is under constant assault from all quarters. Genetically modified crops are spreading worldwide; pests and diseases are evolving rapidly to attack dwindling varieties of plants; multinational corporations are moving to claim utility patents on particular varieties, meaning they own the seed and all its progeny.

The United States Supreme Court declared in December 2001 that it is legal to claim utility patents on plants, making it potentially illegal not just to propagate and sell that seed, but even to save seeds of patented plants from the previous season to plant next season. I like to look at it this way: If you are what you eat, then who owns your food owns you.

Combine these alarming trends with the fact that, as was stated at the Terra Madre World Gathering of Food Communities in 2004, "Today, thirty plant varieties feed 95% of the world's population. In the past century, 250,000 plant varieties have gone extinct, and another plant variety disappears every six hours. Since the beginning of the 20th century, Europe has lost more than 75% of its agricultural biodiversity, whereas the United States have lost 93%…. One third of native cow, sheep and pig breeds has gone extinct or is on the road to extinction."

The world's ecosystem is based on diversity and cannot function without it. As a part of that ecosystem, agriculture cannot function without diversity either. If you doubt that, study just a little about the Irish potato famine to learn what happens if there is only one variety of a plant.

SSE's approach has been to build a network of concerned gardeners and farmers around the world, set some guidelines for the proper preservation of seeds with their genetic makeup intact, and then carefully catalog, store, and distribute these seeds. They are careful never to use all of any particular seed, always saving some in order to make more.

Anyone can buy seeds from SSE, through their print catalog or through their website but if you become a member of the Exchange, you receive access to twice as many varieties of seeds, some 24,000 in all. Many other benefits of joining SSE's eight thousand members are detailed at the website.

If you are ever in the area, I highly recommend a visit to the Heritage Farm in Decorah. SSE operates this small farm that includes the gardens, a historic orchard and a herd of Ancient White Park Cattle. These cattle roamed the British Isles before the time of Christ and are described exactly in ancient Celtic lore. Only about eight hundred are left in the world, and eighty of those are at the Heritage Farm. Visit in July or August to see the gardens in full splendor, or to see the three hundred varieties of garlic hanging to dry. In September or October, stop in to see and taste the best of the orchard's seven hundred nineteenth century apple varieties. That is a lot, but sadly, it is only a fraction of the some eight thousand varieties that were on record in 1899.

By protecting nature's diversity from industrial standardization, Seed Savers Exchange is protecting our heritage and our health. Heirloom seeds carry with them real and vital information about our past, a history that is rich with the wisdom of countless generations. It is no wonder they are recipients of the MacArthur "genius grant," nor that fellow MacArthur recipient and author Gary Paul Nabhan referred to Seed Savers as, "Very possibly the most biodiverse place on the planet."

Garlic Confit

One of the most inspiring things to see at Seed Savers Exchange is all the freshly harvested garlic, hanging row after row in the barn near their historic orchard in late July. The aroma is truly mesmerizing.

A true confit, as described earlier, is a meat - most commonly duck or goose - cooked slowly in its own fat. A garlic confit is a rich delicacy that can be spread on toast, used in a sauce (such as the marinara described later) or simply eaten straight. My wife Kim will eat it like popcorn if given the chance.

To compensate for the lack of fat in garlic with which to make a confit, I use a combination of extra virgin olive oil and grapeseed oil. The reason for the combination is that I like to use the resulting garlic flavored oil for sautés, but most extra virgin oil has a smoking point that is too low to sauté with – it will begin to smoke before it is hot enough to sauté something properly.

Nearly any vegetable-based oil will work for the confit, though. If there is one produced near your home, try that.

> 1 cup whole garlic cloves, peeled
> 1 bay leaf
> 1 sprig fresh rosemary
> 1 pint extra virgin olive oil
> 1 pint grapeseed oil

Place the garlic, bay leaf and rosemary in the bottom of a 3-quart saucepan. Add both oils and place the pan over medium heat. Stir the mixture occasionally. After about 15 minutes, the oil will begin to boil lightly. Adjust the heat and watch carefully because if it boils over a nasty fire could result; that's why we use a 3-quart pan for a 3-pint recipe.

When the cloves turn lightly brown after about 30 minutes, remove the pan from the heat and allow to cool completely. The garlic will cook a little further, and that's a good thing.

After it is cool enough to handle, strain the cloves from the oil. Discard the rosemary and bay leaf, and store the confit in the refrigerator, tightly covered, for up to one week. Reserve the oil for cooking.

Makes 2 pints of garlic-flavored oil, and ¾ cup of garlic confit.

"Slow Food Is Just a Coastal Thing"
Odessa Piper, L'Etoile, and the Myth of the "Fly-Over States."

MADISON, WI – Early each Saturday morning, L'Etoile's Chef and Owner for nearly thirty years, Odessa Piper, perused the abundance outside her front door. Conveniently situated right across Pinckney Street from America's biggest and best producer-only farmers market, L'Etoile has a special advantage. From April to October , three hundred farmers set up stalls around the Wisconsin State Capital Building for the Dane County Farmers Market, which has been in business since 1972. By comparison, New York's Union Square Greenmarket has a mere seventy vendors at the height of their season. Every product at the Dane County Farmers Market must be raised in Wisconsin and be sold by the hands that raised it. That suited Chef Odessa just fine.

Since 1975, Chef Odessa Piper's Madison landmark, L'Etoile, has been demonstrating exactly why it's better to buy local. In May of 2005 she retired, selling the operation to her longtime Chef de Cuisine, Tory Miller, and his sister, Traci Miller. L'Etoile's standards have not changed though: buy what's freshest, buy what's local, and prepare it with love and passion.

Like Chef Odessa before him, Tory Miller gives all credit where credit is due by listing the names of all the local sources on the seasonally rotated menu. One might enjoy local grass-fed Highland Beef from Fountain Prairie, L'Etoile mashed potatoes (like no other, I can assure you), Horseradish-Beauty Heart Radish compound butter, Snug Haven spinach, and red wine jus. Fountain Prairie and Snug Haven are both local farms.

This is not to say that they use exclusively local food - tough to find Wisconsin oranges or olive oil - but they do source everything locally and organically whenever feasible. As Piper once stated on the website: "We believe that respect for nature and all that grows is the beginning of the understanding of good food. We strive to work with ingredients that are cultivated in accordance with their natural cycles, and are grown in their native and adapted soils. We have observed that this cooperation between people and their environment is at the heart of all great cultures, and we strive to cultivate artisan traditions of our own."

Once upon a time the shopping at the Dane County Market was handled by a staff forager, but Chef Tory likes to do it all himself. He enjoys interacting with the farmers, feeling that it keeps him in closer touch with the food coming into his restaurant. Much of the work is done for him, though, by the many farmers who bring their produce right to L'Etoile's back door. Besides those who grow their own crops, there are those who just go out and find them. Often one of L'Etoile's many trusted mushroom hunters will show up out of the blue with a basket full of hen o' the woods, oyster, goat's beard, porcini, or (for just a few weeks in May and June) the coveted morel mushrooms. Most of these are sure to show up on the menu that day, either in the upstairs dining room or in the more casual L'Etoile Café downstairs. Some will be set aside, though, for "puttin' up," as we Heartlanders often call it. Old-fashioned preserving methods, such as drying, canning and curing are *de rigueur* at L'Etoile. Combined with local farmers who use season-extending methods such as hoop houses – like those used by the Snug Haven Spinach folks – L'Etoile has great local produce year-round.

Each afternoon about 3 o'clock the entire staff sits down to what they call "family meal," prepared fresh each day by the talented cooks of L'Etoile, to discuss the evening ahead, the features, and menu changes. All servers' questions are answered, in an effort to avoid confusion later, which could have an impact on the diner's experience. Everything must be clearly understood. This wait staff is not made up of UW college kids merely looking to make some beer money. These are seasoned, well-trained professionals who understand the importance of what Chef Odessa had been doing at L'Etoile all these years.

A review in the *New York Times* by the late great R.W. Apple, Jr., from September, 2004, rightfully heaped praise on Piper, L'Etoile, and the Dane County Market, but it also committed an all-too-common faux pas typical of what I call the bicoastal mentality. At one point Mr. Apple asks the rhetorical question "SO [sic] why Wisconsin?" Granted, the question does not actually ask, word for word, "Why on earth would such a gifted chef want to work in Wisconsin of all places?" but the implication is quite plain and we Midwesterners are accustomed to it. We know that some people from places like New York, Washington DC, San Francisco or L.A. refer to our region as "the fly-over states," and while some other people might be offended by such dismissive treatment, we are not. It is fine if they want to believe there is nothing of value, nothing worth stopping and visiting, in the 13-state triangle that stretches from Ohio to Oklahoma to North Dakota. We have no objection because if those folks think that the Heartland is a wasteland, they are less likely to bring such an attitude here.

So, they can just keep flying over, and we'll wave (we're friendly Midwesterners, after all), as we enter jewels like L'Etoile for another fabulous meal.

Odessa's End of Summer Succotash

When Odessa was the guest chef at the Slow Food Iowa Harvest Dinner in 2005, she did a cooking demonstration in the morning at the Iowa City Farmers' Market as a part of Iowa City's annual Field to Family celebration. Field to Family is a four-day festival of food, literature, symposia, potlucks, mushroom hunts and more, all designed to draw closer connections between the community and its farmers. This innovative reinterpretation of an Heartland classic was one of the dishes she demonstrated.

That night at the dinner, Devotay's then-Sous Chef Paige Haringa and I worked with Odessa to create a marvelous meal of local ingredients, including Warm Smoked Rushing Waters Trout on Silver Dollar Blini with Crème Fraîche, Chilled Melon Soup with Savory Anise Hyssop Biscotti and Fried La Quercia Prosciutto, Wholesome Harvest Organic Chicken Breast with La Quercia Prosciutto-Walnut Compound Butter, served with Roasted Wilson's Orchard "Song of September" Apples Stuffed with Autumn Vegetables and a Sage Cream Sauce and a Penuche Caramel Cream Cake with Autumn Raspberries.

This succotash makes a delightful accompaniment to pork chops or ribs and, like everything else in this book, is best when made with the seasonal ingredients found close to home. Odessa says that the amounts of the ingredients can easily be adjusted to suit your taste.

Edamame has become popular of late as an appetizer in Sushi restaurants, but is actually nothing more than simple soybeans, picked ripe and steamed in their pods with salt. You should of course remove them from the pods before including them here.

> 1 large onion, diced
> ¼ cup olive oil
> 1 smallish summer squash, diced
> 1 cup diced any combination of hot or sweet peppers, blanched edamame,
>   or scallions
> 6 large ears sweet corn: kernels cut from cob
> ½ small musk melon, peeled, seeded, and cut in small 1/2"x 1/2" cubes
> 1 cup loose fresh picked basil, chopped
> 1 lime, zested and juiced (yield 1 ½ tablespoon, add more to taste)
> 4-5 tablespoons unsalted butter cut in cubes
> Sea salt flakes and cracked pepper
> 1/3 cup Riesling (unoaked white wine)

In a large frying pan, sweat onion in olive oil until fragrant and translucent. Add squash, peppers or other vegetables and corn kernels, and cook until they soften, stirring frequently. Add more cooking oil or a splash of extra wine or water if pan is dry. Add melon and cook till it is hot all the way through. Finally add fresh herbs, lime zest, butter, salt and pepper to taste. Serve immediately. Serves 4-6.

Reviving a Local Landmark
The Hotel Donaldson.

FARGO, ND – The Heartland sometimes gets a bum rap as a cold, desolate, cultureless place full of backward old farmers and beat-up pickup trucks. If there were to be a capital of this bone-chillingly bleak remoteness - in this narrow bicoastal mentality - it may well be Fargo, North Dakota. I must confess that for the first four decades of my life, all I knew about the city came from the Coen brothers' movie of the same name and from a word detective on the old PBS children's show *The Electric Company*. I have since had my eyes opened for me, and the Hotel Donaldson (HoDo) is the main reason for my epiphany.

The International Order of Odd Fellows, a fraternity founded in 17th century England to "improve and elevate the character of man" erected the building in 1893. It was their lodge and dance hall until 1915, when it became a hotel for the workers who traveled through on the Northern and Pacific Railroad line. It was something of a derelict by the time Karen Burgum recognized its potential in 2000.

It was no mere facelift that Burgum had in mind. She set out to make the Donaldson a landmark – a center not just of hospitality but also of local and regional food, art and culture. She has succeeded admirably. Each room is a minigallery dedicated to the art of one regional artist, often portraying the landscape of the Great Plains. Exposed brick is everywhere, most notably in the basement wine cellar/tasting room called Stokers. Long-sealed up windows were uncovered to allow sunshine into the restaurant. The old Odd Fellows dance hall, once split into two floors of workman's hotel flats, was recovered well beyond its former splendor

One feels instantly at home here. If I had the means, my master bedroom at home would look almost exactly like the one I experienced at the HoDo one summer's evening, complete with the Ansel Adams-inspired photography of Leo Kim. His silver prints of storm clouds rolling over the grassy prairie can remind you of why digitally produced clipart on a website will never equal the magic of the black and white gelatin prints made one at a time in a darkroom by a dedicated artist.

Of course, the room is just where the HoDo experience starts. What a hotel ought to be, from the fanciest to the simplest, is a place where one can relax, slow down, and feel at home. That is their whole purpose, really – to be surrogate homes. When the Slow Food Manifesto states, "A firm defense of quiet material pleasure is the only way to oppose the universal folly of Fast Life," it does not mean that material pleasure has to be elaborate or expensive. It can be as simple as a good book, or a fresh strawberry, or a favorite teddy bear. It is hard to deny, though, the luxuriant experience of a heated slate tile floor in your bathroom and an oversized down comforter on your king-size bed. All this and more for less than you would pay for a discount hotel in New York City.

I can hear New Yorkers now telling me, "Yes, but that discount hotel is surrounded by New York, not Fargo." True enough, and no one would deny the sheer inexhaustibility of things to see and do in New York. What I am suggesting is not lowering one's standards, but broadening one's palate, and in more ways than one. Not only is the HoDo a splendid gallery, a hip bar, a great restaurant and a very comfortable hotel, it sits in a neighborhood that is experiencing a revival of its own, partially spurred on by the Hotel Donaldson itself. Galleries and boutiques abound. Locally brewed beer is a block away. The Red River of the North is 4 blocks away. There's more in heaven and earth....

Besides being the nickname of the hotel, "HoDo" is the formal name of the restaurant and bar on the street level. The focus is on classical interpretations of regional ingredients, and as Ms. Burgum has done with the hotel in general, Chef Eric Inscho succeeds admirably.

The menu changes seasonally and according to the market, with local twists on what have become traditional American favorites. When I was there, the region's ubiquitous walleye replaced crab, and local horseradish replaced aioli in "Crisp breaded walleye cakes with preserved lemon and horseradish cream." The local lingonberry, a wild cousin of the cranberry with white flowers rather than pink and a rounder fruit, sets off another appetizer: "Pork and lamb meatballs in sour cream gravy with lingonberry coulis." Examples of entrees include Whiskey Creek bison tenderloin (from a farm across the river in Minnesota), with roasted garlic Dijon demi glace and potato croquettes," and "oven-roasted Spring Prairie chicken breast, with caramelized shallot-sherry sauce and truffle mashed potatoes."

The Hotel Donaldson's use of local art and local ingredients, tied with its support of the community around it and its sense of history, all follow one clear and sustainable principle: use the abundance found around you, and use it with passionate respect.

Wild Rice Burgers

The Hotel Donaldson is just an hour and a half from the White Earth Reservation, where the traditional Manoomin wild rice is still hand-harvested by the Ojibwe people, using traditional, time-tested methods. Real hand parched, "Manoomin" wild rice cooks much faster and with less water than its domesticated counterparts.

Chef Eric uses the rice to make these earthy vegetarian burgers for the hotel's eclectic restaurant, HoDo.

½ cup raw green lentils
½ cup pearled barley
1 cup Manoomin Wild Rice
5 cups water
1 carrot, minced
1 celery stalk, minced
½ medium yellow onion, minced
2 tablespoons olive oil
1 cup dried shiitake mushrooms
1 tablespoon fresh sage, minced
1 tablespoon fresh thyme, chopped
1 tablespoon fresh parsley, chopped
2 tablespoons soy sauce
¼ cup cornstarch

Cook lentils, barley and rice each separately in a 1:2 ratio (food:water). Make sure the rice is fully bloomed (cooked enough to open up).

Meanwhile, sauté the carrots, celery, and onion in olive oil until tender (do not brown). Soak the mushrooms in 1 cup of boiling water until tender, then drain and reserve the liquid. Dice the mushrooms.

Preheat oven to 350°

In one bowl, combine the vegetables, barley, rice, mushrooms, and herbs. Separately, combine cooked lentils with the soy sauce, mushroom broth, and cornstarch. Puree the lentil mixture in a food processor, then fold into the vegetable-rice mix. Taste and adjust for salt.

Gently form the mixture into 6 ounce patties and arrange on a parchment-lined sheetpan. Bake at 350° for 30 minutes. Cool and store, covered, in the refrigerator until service.

Before service, sauté in olive oil until lightly browned and heated through. Serve in any way that you might serve ordinary hamburgers. Makes 6-8 patties.

"New York Didn't Need Another Restaurant"

Chef MJ Adams Comes Home to Cook.

RAPID CITY, SD – Growing up with your grandmother in Mitchell, South Dakota, may not seem like the launching pad to owning a fine restaurant and being featured in *Gourmet* magazine (among others), but it did teach MJ Adams the importance of roots, of placeness, of home.

With twelve years in New York City, a degree from the French Culinary Institute in Soho, and several restaurant experiences under her apron strings (including winning accolades from the *New York Times* while chef at Seasons in Brooklyn), Chef MJ returned to her native Great Plains to create great food from local ingredients.

Her intent was to rescue this one little corner of the world from the drudgery of repetitious, mundane fare by creating a classical bakery with modern adaptations, providing both savory and sweet pastries as well as gourmet foods and the soul-enriching touches of her grandmother. The usual chains were all that there was to choose from in this tourist-driven town near Mt. Rushmore, and Adams wanted to offer something a little more interesting, more genuine - what she described as the "pure enjoyment of creating and consuming food made from scratch, using local and organically grown ingredients."

She found an empty storefront in downtown Rapid City and set about realizing the dream. She called it the Corn Exchange, after a Brooklyn bank building she once dreamed of converting to a restaurant. Initially conceived as a bakery, it was not well received at first. Locals did not seem to understand the food, the portions, or the prices. She was, as one critic observed, "serving scones to a sticky-bun crowd."

Then, things got worse. A fire, started in a nearby business that also devastated most of the city block, consumed the Corn Exchange. Adams' marriage collapsed, and her dream had become a nightmare. Alone on the prairie, she wondered if her desire to bring homemade, genuine food back to the region could possibly be rekindled. South Dakotans seemed to have forgotten what real food tasted like. Were they doomed to the homogeneous mediocrity of the cookie-cutter chains?

Metaphors like "darkest before the dawn," and "Phoenix-like" come to mind when discussing the miracles that occurred next. The very same community that had shunned the Corn Exchange before the fire rallied around MJ Adams. They held a benefit to raise money, and then-Senator Tom Daschle arranged some federal disaster assistance. The oddball bakery that nobody understood suddenly was a point of civic pride and a rallying point for people who cared about food. The Corn Exchange was reborn in a nearby, larger space, this time as a full service restaurant

Since then, Adams and her crew have built it into the jewel of the Black Hills. She has received national attention in magazines such as *Gourmet* and *Elle*. People in Rapid City have become proud that their town could lay claim to having what *Gourmet* called "the best restaurant between Minneapolis and Denver."

There are still many challenges to providing local food in Rapid City, to be sure. The short growing season limits the farmers' market season to July through September, but with diligence Adams has created a network of farmers throughout the region she can rely on to provide delicious, sustainably grown produce and meat. Organic, farm-raised trout, pheasant, and quail are all now as readily available to the Corn Exchange as South Dakota's signature bison. Hoop houses and other season-extending techniques have made the local produce available for a larger portion of the year.

All this is taken in by Adams and her all-woman kitchen crew (still a rarity in the restaurant business) and transformed into scrumptious, classical fare that displays the bounty and placeness of the Heartland that Adams set out to highlight. Greens and chicken come from Smithwick Gardens, goat cheese from Haystack Mountain in Colorado, blue cheese from the famous Iowa cheesemaker Maytag, buffalo meat from the Intertribal Buffalo Council of South Dakota or the 777 Ranch in Hermosa, Angus beef from Deiter Brothers in Faulkton.

Adams knows well the symbiotic relationship that occurs when a restaurant supports its own community. "New York didn't need another restaurant," she said, but Rapid City did, and she answered the call. What's next, she believes, is for more culinary professionals to bring the ethic of local, sustainable, slow food to all parts of the country that have no variety to choose from.

When you think about it, all great revolutions have started in the countryside.

Bison Empanadas with Chimichuri Sauce

The Corn Exchange originally opened as a bakery, and since Chef MJ's then-husband was from South America, she wanted to mix some of his culinary traditions with South Dakota's signature meat, bison. These savory turnovers were the result.

To reconstitute sun-dried tomatoes, place them in a saucepan with enough water to cover. Bring to a quick boil, then set aside for 15 minutes. Drain and cool.

Fleur de sel is a special kind of sea salt, harvested from the reeds along Europe's Atlantic coast (especially Brittany). Kosher salt can be a reasonable, though by no means identical, substitution.

For the Dough:
3 cups white, unbleached flour
½ cup cold butter
¼ cup lard
¼ cup ice cold water
1 whole egg
Fleur de sel

For the Filling:
2 T. of Olive oil
1 medium onion, mince
2 garlic cloves minced
2 stalked of celery, mince
2 carrots, peeled, mince
2 pounds fresh ground bison meat
½ cups green olives, sliced
½ cup reconstituted sun-dried tomatoes, chopped
4 hard-boiled eggs, peeled and chopped
Salt and pepper for seasoning

For the Sauce:
1 cup parsley, chopped
1 tablespoon garlic, finely minced
¼ cup red wine vinegar
¾ cup extra virgin olive oil
1 teaspoon red pepper flakes

To maker the dough, place flour in bowl, and cut in butter and lard. Slowly work water into flour mixture with left hand, checking for moisture content with right hand. Depending on the temperature of the kitchen and the temperature of your hand, you may need less or more cold water. Do not overwork. Let rest, covered by a damp cotton towel, for 15-30 minutes

Meanwhile, heat a large sauté pan. Add the olive oil. Toss in the onion, garlic, celery, and carrots. Sauté for 5-15 minutes on medium heat till lightly browned. Add the ground buffalo, cook to medium well (it will cook more once in the oven inside the dough), breaking up with a fork while cooking. Add olives, sun-dried tomatoes and taste for seasoning, then adjust as needed.

Remove the filling from stove and let it cool completely. Add the eggs and mix ingredients thoroughly.

Preheat oven to 400°

Divide the dough into 12 portions and roll each into a circle, about ¼ inch thick. Cover with the damp cotton towel and let rest again for 15 minutes.

Brush the perimeter of one circle with water, scoop about ¼ cup of filling onto one side, then fold in half and press the two edges firmly together, crimping if desired, or place on a baking sheet and with a end of the fork tines, press the edges together. Brush with beaten egg. Lightly sprinkle fleur de sel on top of each empanada. Bake at 400°for 25 minutes or until browned.

While the empanadas are baking, make the sauce by combining the parsley, garlic, vinegar, olive oil and red pepper flakes. Whisk well.

Serve the Empanadas at room temperature or right out of the oven on a platter with a bowl of the Chimichuri sauce on the side. Makes 12 empanadas.

Season to Season

Lucia's Restaurant and Wine Bar.

MINNEAPOLIS, MN – In 1985, no one in the Twin Cities of Minneapolis and St. Paul, Minnesota, had even considered the idea of a restaurant that was guided by the seasons. No one, that is, until third generation Minnesotan Lucia Watson returned to her home state to shake things up a bit.

After great success in the kitchen of L'Auberge in Middleburg, Virginia, she ran her own catering firm in Minneapolis, then opened Lucia's Restaurant on West 31st Street in the neighborhood known as Uptown in 1985. Her passionate devotion to local, seasonal, sustainable cuisine can be seen on every weekly menu at Lucia's. For lunch one day you might enjoy Fisher Farm's pork tenderloin with hoisin - ginger glaze and cous cous, then come back for dinner and have parmesan-crusted chicken breast with salsa verde and braised white beans. A week later, the menu will be different again. It's all in keeping with Watson's philosophy – fresh is best.

The décor of Lucia's is elegant, but unpretentious and comfortable, like the food. One is just as comfortable having a romantic dinner here as having a casual night out with friends. Artwork is classy and minimalist, and fresh seasonal flowers adorn each room. There is a quiet bustle to the busiest Saturday night which affords an ambience that is at once stylish and relaxing.

For more than twenty years, these ideas have kept Lucia's at the forefront of the fickle big-city restaurant world. Operating a restaurant on this model, with weekly changing menus and every ingredient feasible from local sources, is perhaps the most challenging way to do it. There is no doubt that it would be easier to simply call one harried salesperson, a regional representative of one of the huge food distribution companies, arrange for all your ingredients to arrive on the back of a truck the next day. It is often cheaper, too. That is why a vast majority of America's restaurants, from big chains to small, independent diners do it that way, and why all their dishes tend to taste alike.

There are more reasons to shun this commercialized method in favor of the local and the seasonal than simply the mundane flavors in the chain restaurants. What appears less expensive on the face of it hides severe hidden costs to everyone. My home state of Iowa for example, despite being an agricultural state, imports about 94 percent of its food and that food travels an average of 1500 miles, according to Iowa State University's Leopold Center for Sustainable Agriculture. The vegetables are picked and the meat processed by often-underpaid, often-undocumented migrant workers. The same is true for the rest of the states included in this book and for most of the states in the Union.

That importation siphons capital from the state. It forces produce to be picked before it is ripe, costing nutritional value. The packaging and transportation have a massive impact on the environment, and again nutrients are lost as produce sits in trucks and on train cars. The processing, especially the addition of sweeteners and preservatives, combines with all those lost nutrients and leads to a heavy burden on our healthcare system. In the meat processing plants, according to *Fast Food Nation* author Eric Schlosser, one in three workers is injured to the point of hospitalization every year. All this only scrapes the surface of the hidden cost of cheap food.

Lucia Watson has twice been nominated for the prestigious James Beard Award as Best Chef in the Midwest, yet she is still as down to earth as it gets. She loves the North Woods, where she learned to cook at her grandmother Lulu's apron strings. Her ardor for the food of the Upper Midwest led her to collaborate with Beth Dooley in 1995 to write *Savoring the Seasons of the Northern Heartland*, a dog-eared copy of which sits on my cookbook shelf to this day.

Owning and operating this successful restaurant in a historic Minneapolis neighborhood is not enough for Watson. She has served on the board of directors of the Chefs' Collaborative, an organization of culinary professionals with goals and aspirations very much in line with those of Slow Food, and she has also been active with the Women Chefs and Restaurateurs. She has served as the board chair of the Youth Farm and Market Project, which endeavors to teach kids about the importance of sustainability and how to produce food in an urban environment.

Watson became quite the Francophile while studying the French language at the University of Minnesota. Now, if you don't find her cooking in the small, orderly kitchen of Lucia's, then she is likely to be in her refurbished home in Brittany. There she unwinds and gathers inspiration to carry back to Minneapolis, where people still happily line up to sample what she has found in the farms and forests of the northern Heartland.

Puree of Watercress Soup

Diners at Lucia's delight in seeing this luscious soup appear on the menu in the spring. It is one of those wonderful soups that can be just as good chilled as it is served piping hot.

Homemade chicken stock is irreplaceable, but if necessary, one could use water. The depth of flavor will not be the same. Canned stocks and bouillon cubes are all too salty.

2 tablespoons butter
1 cup peeled and diced russet potatoes
¼ cup diced celery
¼ cup diced onion
1 cup chicken stock
½ cup milk
¼ cup heavy cream
1 bunch watercress, stems removed
1 ½ teaspoons salt
¼ teaspoon white pepper
A splash of dry sherry, if desired
Croutons or crumbled blue cheese to garnish.

Melt the butter in a large stockpot over low flame. Place the potatoes, celery, and onion in the pot and cover. Cook, stirring occasionally, until vegetables are very soft. Do not allow them to brown. Add the stock, milk, and cream, turn up the heat and bring to a boil, then turn back down to a simmer.

After the soup has simmered for about 45 minutes, toss in the watercress, and puree. An immersible blender is very handy for this, but a standard one will work as well, if you puree it in batches. For a very smooth texture, pass the pureed soup through a fine mesh strainer.

Garnish with croutons or a crumble of blue cheese, Yields 4-5 one cup servings.

COMMUNITY AND OUTREACH

"There is more to life than increasing its speed."
-Mahatma Gandhi

Securing Food

The Nebraska Sustainable Agriculture Society and Community CROPS.

Lincoln, NE – The wise folks at the Global Resource Action Center for the Environment (GRACE) define sustainable agriculture as "farming that provides a secure living for farm families; maintains the natural environment and resources; supports the rural community; and offers respect and fair treatment to all involved, from farm workers to consumers to the animals raised for food."

This idea has been gaining ground – literally – and the Nebraska Sustainable Agriculture Society has been leading the way. Since 1976, NSAS has helped farmers and consumers make informed decisions that have positive effects on the health of their families and their land. Composed of rural and urban consumers, market gardeners, educators, and of course farmers raising a fantastic array of goods, they hold frequent conferences and workshops on subjects such as transitioning to certified organic production and seed saving, and have farm tours and field days for their members to build networks and learn sustainable farming practices. NSAS reaches out to the non-farmer as well. They developed a list of "Seven ways you can change the world…by eating!" It is written for Nebraskans, but the lessons apply worldwide:

1. Shop at a farmers' market. When you buy food from a farmers' market, you directly support a farm family AND the money you spend on that food is likely to stay in a Nebraska community. Produce from the farmers' market is fresher, tastier, and more nutritious than produce from California, Florida, or Mexico. Shopping at a farmers' market is good for you and Nebraska's economy.

2. Buy chicken, beef, pork, or eggs directly from a farmer. When you know the farmer who grows your food, you can ask him or her what kinds of hormones or antibiotics are used and avoid eating additives that you don't want. Farm-fresh meat and eggs taste better than anything you can get at the grocery store, and the farmer

is able to capture more of the food dollar by selling his or her product directly to you.

3. Grow a garden. Even if you only have space for a tomato plant in a container or some herbs on your windowsill, growing some of your own food makes a statement about the kind of food system you want. Growing food helps your kids understand where their food comes from and appreciate the work it takes to put food on the table. Starting a community garden can give all people a chance to grow some of their own food and improve their health, nutrition, and standard of living.

4. Ask your grocer to carry locally grown food. Nebraska family farmers raise meat, produce, eggs, honey, dairy and grain products, yet most of what we buy at the grocery store comes from out of state. By creating consumer demand for healthy, local foods, you create new markets for Nebraska family farmers.

5. Eat more "slow" food. Fast foods are usually highly processed and not very good for you. The mega-corporations and chains that process and prepare fast foods often do not pay their employees well, and a lot of energy is used to process and transport this food. The extra time spent preparing and eating fresh meat, fruit, grains, and vegetables can be valuable family time that would be lost if you grabbed a burger at a fast food chain.

6. Join a Community Supported Agriculture farm. Community Supported Agriculture, or CSA, builds partnerships between farmers and consumers. CSA members purchase shares in a farm at the beginning of the growing season to meet the farmer's operating expenses. In return, these members receive a share of the farm's produce throughout the growing season. CSA farms often hold festivals and educational events for their members.

7. Choose food grown in a way that's good for the environment, people, communities, and your health. "Sustainably" raised foods are grown using agricultural management practices such as crop rotations and intensive grazing to control pests, build soil, and prevent disease in animals. When you buy organic or sustainably raised foods, you are doing your part to keep our water clean, encourage wildlife, and keep our soil healthy. You also know that farm workers were not exposed to potentially hazardous chemicals and that animals were treated humanely.

Perhaps the most exciting NSAS project is "Community Combining Resources, Opportunities, and People for Sustainability. (CROPS)" Begun in 2003 by Andy Witkowski, and now managed with a board led by Ingrid Kirst, Community CROPS is a gardening project targeting mainly immigrants, refugees and low-income families in the Lincoln area. Beginning with just one garden, it now has four of them, plus a four-acre farm. At each garden, participants can tend plots of their own vegetables, learn from each other and from the CROPS volunteers, and have a clean, inexpensive, reliable source of fresh food.

Many people grow foods native to their homelands, and it is not uncommon to see a Brazilian garden next to a Japanese garden, then a Bosnian couple tending their plot next to a man from Sudan. Participants have included immigrants and refugees from the former Yugoslavia, Indonesia, Japan, Hong Kong, Peru, Brazil, Sudan, Iraq (Yzedis), Guatemala, El Salvador, and Mexico. It is very hard not to feel at home, even in a strange new land, when you are tending your very own garden.

NSAS's mission is to promote agriculture and food systems that build healthy land, people, communities and quality of life, for present and future generations. There is no doubt that they are actively accomplishing that mission, and living up to the true definition of sustainable agriculture.

Gazpacho Andaluz

My restaurant's food is primarily Spanish cuisine. So when July rolls around and my wife Kim comes in from the Devotay Gardens with an armload of the summer's bounty, the whole place gets in a gazpacho kind of mood.

This recipe, made in the style of Andalusia on the southwest coast of Spain, is the style most people expect when they order gazpacho. It is simple, but the preparation of each of the ingredients, before they go in the blender, can take a little time for the less-experienced. It is well worth it though. There is nothing more refreshing on a hot summer afternoon than this soup and a chilled glass of dry sherry.

3 pounds tomatoes, peel, seed & dice
1 yellow onion, diced
2 green pepper, cored & diced
2 roasted red peppers
4 cloves garlic, peeled
4 white bread slices, crusts removed
2 1/2 cups tomato juice
6 tablespoons extra virgin olive oil
4 tablespoons red wine vinegar
salt and pepper, to taste
ice cubes, at service
1 each red and green bell peppers, minced
1 onion, minced
2 hard-boiled egg, minced
2 cups croutons

In a large bowl, mix together the peeled, seeded and diced tomato, with the onion, peppers, garlic, white bread, tomato juice, olive oil, vinegar, salt and pepper.

In several batches, depending on the size of your food processor or blender, puree this mixture until smooth. Chill it completely, 3 hours to overnight.

Serve in chilled bowls, garnished with an ice cube, the minced peppers and onion, the chopped egg and the crouton. Serves 8.

Food Within Reach

Laura Dowd and Local Foods Connection.

Iowa City, IA – in 1995, Laura Dowd was at a crossroads. She wanted to provide organic vegetables for her husband as part of his cancer recovery plan, but money was tight. She decided to pay for the vegetables through farm work, so she volunteered with Susan Jutz and Simone Delaty of Local Harvest, a Community Supported Agriculture (CSA) system in Johnson County.

A CSA is a little like a magazine subscription for farm fresh food. Participants buy a "share" in the early spring, paying up front for food they will receive throughout the season. In this perfect win-win scenario, the farmers get the cash they need to get the season started well, and the families who join get a box of fresh, seasonal produce each week, all season long. Here in Iowa, that is around twenty weeks of radishes, greens, sweet peas, zucchini, potatoes, tomatoes, squash and much more. Local Harvest also offers hearth-baked bread, fresh-cut flowers, lamb, pork and eggs. Everything they offer is organic.

Soon Dowd, Jutz and Delaty were discussing the challenges involved in putting local, organic food within reach of single-parent households and other economically disadvantaged members of the community. From these discussions, Local Foods Connection (LFC) was born in 1999. Originally called Adopt-a-Family, the idea was to solicit donations from CSA members and the general public; then this money would be used to buy CSA shares for qualifying families. Families and farmers both get the support they need; it's another win-win, like the CSAs themselves.

Though by no means easy, the work has paid off for LFC and for the people Dowd affectionately calls her families. Today LFC is a lot more than a charity that raises money and hands out food. Its more than 50 office volunteers doing clerical and educational work, and 225 more volunteers who work with five different area farms. Rather than paying these hardworking helpers (including several from the University of Iowa service fraternity Alpha Kappa Psi), CSAs provide charity credit toward food purchases, which LFC distributes to its clients and that is only the beginning. LFC educates families about cooking, nutrition and the advantages of buying locally.

In 2005 when the New Pioneer Co-op in Iowa City sent dividend checks to its members, they included a letter with each check requesting that the members sign these checks over to LFC. The response was so overwhelming that an extremely grateful Ms. Dowd said, "This will change the charity." In 2006, when the Co-op's dividend program was repeated, donations more than tripled.

One of her families (who asked to remain anonymous) emigrated from the West African country of Burkina Faso in 2000. With one parent in graduate school at the University of Iowa and three boys to feed, the other parent's hard work as a nursing assistant wasn't enough. With the help of Dayna Ballantyne, director of the Johnson County Crisis Center Food Bank, they met Dowd and learned of the Local Foods Connection program.

The family loved the food and appreciated help with the unfamiliar vegetables (they liked the zucchini, but not the beets, both of which were new to them). They particularly enjoyed visiting Susan Jutz's pastoral ZJ Farm in Solon, Iowa. These visits are required of all participating families, and Dowd says that it is sometimes difficult to get the families to go to the farms, but once there, it is even tougher to get them to leave. This family enjoyed the visit so much they returned twice with friends, even held a cookout there, and say they look forward to returning soon.

Working with LFC has taught all the families the importance of buying locally. Many now shop the Iowa City Farmers' Market regularly. They've learned that buying locally can be far less expensive (in real terms – when you account for the impact of "cheap" food), and far more nutritious than buying the heavily shipped and fertilized food in the grocery stores. LFC educates its families, volunteers, and donors that the shelf price of food should not be a primary factor in deciding whether or not to purchase it.

The families and the farmers have formed a bond and Dowd feels it is important to emphasize the knowledge that hard work is what creates this food. This bond between the farmer and the urban dweller also helps slow urban sprawl, because people become aware: No farmers, no food.

From its humble beginnings as a dream shared by Dowd, Jutz and Delaty, LFC has grown to include eighteen families and 10 farms in 2006, including not just Local Harvest CSA, but also Choice Earth, Gooseberry Hill, Oak Hill Acres, Scattergood Farms, Friendly Farms, and Fae Ridge Farms. Calvin and Judy Yoder of Echo Dell in Kalona, Iowa, supply chickens, and each family receives a Slow Food Ark USA-registered heritage turkey for Thanksgiving from Henry and Ila Miller, also of Kalona. A four-person LFC Board of Directors makes sure everything runs smoothly.

Most of the families are single-parent, and are directed to the charity by the Crisis Center, the Shelter House, Goodwill, United Action for Youth, Big Brothers/Big Sisters, and the Women's Resource and Action Center, all amazing and hard-working charities in their own right.

Dowd looks forward to being able to help even more families discover the value and nutrition of fresh, local food.

Laura's Tabouli

Laura writes: "This recipe is appropriate for Local Foods Connection in many ways. The tomatoes, cucumbers, onions, garlic, mint and parsley are all in season at the same time (if you tend your herb plants properly). The charity encourages people to learn seasonal eating, so they can enjoy vegetables at their peak of ripeness and taste, and purchase food grown by local farmers. This tabouli does not require cooking, so it is fun and easy to make on a hot August day. The meal is delicious, so this recipe is a great way to introduce new grains and legumes to people, and make them anxious to try more."

1 heaping cup bulgur
1 cup cold water
½ cup fresh lemon juice
2/3 cup extra virgin olive oil
1 cup coarsely chopped fresh mint leaves
1 cup coarsely chopped parsley
½ cup finely diced red onion
2 teaspoon minced garlic
1 teaspoon black pepper
1/2 teaspoon salt
4 ripe plum tomatoes, diced
1 large cucumber, peeled, seeded and diced
1 cup cooked Great Northern White Beans
Fresh mint leaves to garnish

Combine bulgur, water, lemon juice and 1/3 cup of the olive oil. The lemon juice "cooks" the bulgur. Mix well. Set aside in refrigerator for a half of a day to overnight. The longer you set it aside, the less crunchy the bulgur will be.

Add mint, parsley, onion, garlic, pepper, salt, and remaining 1/3 cup of the olive oil. Add tomatoes, cucumber, and beans.

Set the tabouli aside at room temperature for 30 minutes before serving. Garnish with fresh mint. Serves 4 as an entrée salad or 6-8 as a side dish.

Mother Knows Best

Bryan Welch and *Mother Earth News.*

LAWRENCE, KS – Halfway between Topeka and the Missouri River, along the I-70 corridor that connects Topeka to Kansas City, sits the agreeable little college town of Lawrence. Besides being home to the University of Kansas Jayhawks and a fantastic microbrewery called Free State Brewing, it is also the home of Ogden Publications publisher Bryan Welch's new farm. Here, with the towers of KU in the distance, he practices what his flagship magazine *Mother Earth News* preaches: sustainable, self-reliant living.

On the day I visited Welch, he had just completed a review of eight different farm tractors for a story in an upcoming issue of *Mother*. He and his staff hadn't yet decided which performed better, but their devoted readers would know soon enough.

As we visited his grass-fed Angus cows, who like the other animals on his farm had never needed to see a veterinarian, we discussed what the magazine's mission is, and who the readers are. *Mother*'s target audience is the folks who are interested in self-reliance and "conscientious living." In any particular issue one might find a feature article about solar power, another on how to build a large desk cheaply and still another on the glories of sweet corn.

All of Ogden's publications, from *Mother* to their new *Herb Companion* and the recently acquired *Utne Reader*, to old standbys like *Cappers*, *Gas Engine Magazine* and *Grit* (coincidentally I used to deliver *Grit* door to door, as a nine-year-old kid, in response to an ad in the back of a comic book), convey the same quiet, sturdy, Kansas self-determination that gave rise to the Populist party more than years ago. Farmers then wanted the same things farmers want now: some land, some sun, some rain, and a fair price.

Though the party affiliation of a majority of Kansans may be different today, their passion for self-reliance is as strong as ever, and *Mother Earth News* helps them and people all over North America live in ways that are health conscious, energy independent, more productive and less harmful to earth. Raising food for yourself and your neighbors is one of the ways *Mother* encourages this independence.

Welch says that the simplest way to live at a slower pace is to "go find good food that's grown by conscientious people and buy a lot of it." He and his magazine recognize the importance of knowing where your food comes from and teaching that knowledge to our children. One *Mother* article, by Umut Newbury, related the story of Chez Panisse Chef/Owner Alice Waters, and her efforts to make sustainable cuisine part of the curriculum in the Berkeley, California, school district. That effort has been so successful, in fact, that Waters is working to take the plan nationwide, and it is the main thrust of Slow Food in Schools. It has begun, using the Chez Panisse Foundation's Edible Schoolyard at the Martin Luther King, Jr. Middle School in Berkeley as a role model, with the formation of more than twenty school gardens around the country (and more sprouting up all the time).

In the Heartland, for example, you can find these gardens at Crossroads Elementary in St. Paul, Minnesota, and at the Elizabeth Tate High School in Iowa City, Iowa. Their purpose is to help children understand that carrots come from the earth, not the grocery store and that a tomato is not supposed to taste like wet cardboard. In the meantime kids learn about sustainability, hard work, respect, self-reliance, fortitude, and gratitude. They also learn math, history, biology, health, chemistry and on and on. Any subject that can be taught in school, after all, can be taught in a garden.

Mother Earth News teaches these same values in every issue. Bryan Welch lives them on his farm. His Angus cattle, Katahdin sheep, goats, catfish, chickens and mule all benefit from his attention to the principles of stewardship. Some of the easiest, and occasionally even the cheapest, methods of living a slow life are revealed in the pages of *Mother Earth News*. Looking for a way to water your livestock automatically without worrying about it freezing in our harsh Heartland winters? *Mother* can show you. Want to learn which bugs are beneficial for your organic garden? *Mother* can teach you. Would you like to extend your tomato harvest into December in your own, earth-sheltered greenhouse? *Mother* will tell you how.

It is refreshing to know that in a country that can so easily become fascinated with pop-culture minutiae, that can spend months obsessing over the trial of a favorite celebrity, there are still places where one can glean useful information with which to lead a slower, more harmonious rhythm of life. As Welch once wrote in his blog, "We [humans] may ultimately fail to achieve our potential. We may spoil our own nest. We could ruin our own habitat. Then we would, like other species before us, precipitate our own extinction, victims of our own success. But it's miraculous, in some sense, that we can even consider it, that we can acknowledge the negative consequences of our prosperity. No other creature does, so far as we can tell.

"And we do succeed, to various degrees, in living a little more gently than we might."

Grilled Steak, Argentine Style

Offering more of a method that a recipe per se for the type of grass-fed beef he raises, Bryan writes: "My family and I have visited Argentina twice. We were inspired by the devotion to grass-fed meats. Not only have they resisted the contemporary drive toward feed lot agriculture, they are positively militant about the positive flavor qualities of grass-finished beef. They eat it with very little garnish, cooked as simply as possible:

"For all cuts of grass-fed, dry-aged meat, defrost the meat slowly. Resist the temptation to microwave! If you must, put it in a watertight bag and float it in running cold water until it's thoroughly defrosted.

"For tender cuts of beef, no marination or special preparation is necessary. Make sure the fire on your grill or griddle is turned up high. Cooking the exterior of the steak quickly helps seal the juices inside. If you prefer a steak more thoroughly cooked, you can move it to the side to finish cooking (over lower heat) after the surface has been quickly seared. Season afterward with salt, pepper, or spicy Argentine Chimichuri sauce.

"If your cut of meat comes from a less tender part of the animal, you may want to marinate the meat in a salt and vinegar solution for 12 hours or so. However when my animals are butchered before the end of their first breeding season, and the carcasses are dry-aged for at least two weeks, I've never needed to marinate any cut."

Saving the Earth by Saving the Soil
Terra Brockman and The Land Connection.

CONGERVILLE, IL – Throughout this book I've discussed the importance of passion in regard to food. In the tiny town of Congerville, Illinois, Terra Brockman is demonstrating how that single-minded passion can change the world, one acre at a time. Her organization, The Land Connection (TLC), has set about saving the rich soil of Illinois and the farms and families on it. Brockman grew up in this part of the Heartland, traveled the world for decades and now is happily rooted back in her home state, teaching the values of connection to the land that TLC espouses.

In 2001, Brockman noticed a "For Sale" sign in the corner of a nearby farm in Woodford County. After a little investigating, she found that it was being sold for development because the elderly owners needed the money for their medicine. Brockman sprang into action, incorporated a non-profit, and placed a bid. It was accepted. All she needed now was the money. Through the generosity of many committed citizens they raised the money and closed on the property in February of 2002. Within just a couple months, they had a family, the Kaebs, settling in and renewing the farm.

In just a few short years TLC has become a powerhouse educational enterprise, helping connect farmers, restaurants and individual consumers with each other and the land. Meanwhile, it has purchased and adapted to organic food production nearly fifty acres of land that had been slated for urban development and helped new farmers begin projects on that land. At the same time, TLC has assisted dozens of area family farmers in direct marketing to restaurants and consumers and helped others make the transition to organic methods.

Terra's vision for TLC is a deceptively simple one. She said TLC is working to create a food system that is truly sustainable, "one that enables farmers to make a living without handouts, and one that allows them to pass their farm on to the next generation. One that connects food producers and consumers in a direct and compelling way. One that preserves and enhances the quality of the soil, air, and water on which all life depends." That issue of passing on the farm is a serious one. According to the Census Bureau, only 25 percent of America's farm ownership is inheritance, and that number has been shrinking. The way of life that created civilization, small family farms that sustain the community, is vanishing.

At its core, TLC is about helping farmers, old and new, to farm in an environmentally and economically viable way. This is done through a huge variety of projects funded through grants, private donations, and entrepreneurial endeavors such as The Land Connection's cooperative CSA.

TLC's partnership with Slow Food USA and the University of Illinois helped create IllinoisFarmDirect.org, a very useful and user-friendly online catalog of local food sources in the state. They also teamed up with Farm Aid for their twentieth anniversary concert in 2005, which helped raise money and awareness of the plight of the family farmer. Terra led a Champaign to Chicago Good Food and Farm Caravan to kick off the big concert, conducting farm tours, demonstrations, potlucks, and seminars all along the "food route" from central Illinois to Tinley Park, near Chicago. The Farm Aid truck was loaded with fresh food from family farms at every stop along the way, and this food was then prepared for the musicians and crew at the concert. An enormous undertaking in its own right, the caravan reached thousands with its message of sustainability and fresh, great-tasting local food.

Many of the farmers and related businesses that TLC has helped are now thriving. For instance, the Tharp family "graduated" from their year of raising sheep and cattle on TLC land, and now have a small farm of their own in southern Illinois. In 2005, the Weigand family and the Lawrence family raised organic sheep, chickens, turkeys, and hogs on TLC land. The Land Connection facilitates farmer-chef connections that have enabled many area farmers to sell to restaurants, including Cheryl Webb and Floyd Johnson, who sell their pasture-raised chickens to Chicago restaurants. Also in 2005, through an Illinois AgriFirst grant that TLC solicited, Bittner's Meat Locker in Eureka became the first (and only) USDA certified organic meat locker in the state. The next infrastructure project that TLC will address is the lack of chicken and waterfowl processors in the state.

In 2006 TLC began working to create a delivery infrastructure for the increasing amounts of locally raised organic food. "We need a more organized system that involves a computerized inventory. We need regular truck deliveries and a food collection point," says Brockman. This would enable the small local farmers to provide food to restaurants, groceries, and consumers around the state, especially in the major metropolitan areas like Chicago. In this way, those people could import their food from another county instead of half way across the country or halfway around the world. The result: fresher, better tasting, more healthful food and stronger, more prosperous farms.

Just imagine how much better our food would be if there were Terra Brockmans working in every part of every state in the Heartland. The good news is that there are many, and more all the time. Brockman repeatedly quotes Margaret Mead on the TLC website, pointing out that one should "Never doubt that a small group of thoughtful, committed citizens can change the world; indeed, it's the only thing that ever has."

Devotay Marinara

While not technically a marinara according to the strictest Italian food taxonomists, it is nonetheless what this sauce has come to be called since I created it in Devotay's very early days. It is an incredible versatile sauce, used on its own over pasta or in lasagna, pureed and used in Kathy Eckhouse's pasta rolls (see recipe pg 64) as the basis for other sauces, and even as a soup we call Roasted Garlic Tomato Cream. We make it in five-gallon batches at the restaurant, but of course this recipe is meant for a much smaller scale.

It uses many of the things that are coming out of the farms that the Land Connection helps protect - tomatoes, onions, garlic, fennel, herbs – to create a dish packed with rich, savory flavor, although almost devoid of fat (unlike its authentic Italian counterpart).

The tomatoes in this recipe are Amish Paste, an heirloom variety prevalent in the Heartland, but any meaty, dense, low-moisture variety will suffice. The imported, canned, San Marzano variety are a reasonable substitution if tomatoes are out of season, but please do not use the hard, mealy, pink things that pass for tomatoes in some groceries in January. Their lack of flavor turns this magnificent sauce into a wasted effort.

To peel and seed tomatoes, follow this quick, simple method: Bring a gallon of salted water to a boil. While it heats, make an ice bath by putting a large bowl of water and plenty of ice next to the stove. Core the tomatoes (a little gadget called a tomato shark is handy for this) then using a sharp pairing knife cut an "X" in the bottom of each tomato, then plunge them, two or three at a time, into the boiling, salted water for about 45 seconds. The skins will become very loose. Use tongs to remove them and plunge immediately into your ice bath. This makes them easier to handle and stops the cooking process cold, as it were. It is called "shocking" the tomatoes. Once they are cool enough to handle, a minute or so, use your pairing knife to peel away the skin starting at the point of the "X." Repeat for all your tomatoes.

To seed them, simply cut them in half, and then with the cut side down over a bowl or the sink, gently squeeze the tomato half and the seeds will come pouring out.

This sauce can be served immediately, but is best if made a day ahead, then cooled and reheated.

> 2 tablespoons fresh parsley, stemmed and chopped
> 2 tablespoons fresh rosemary, chopped fine
> 2 tablespoons fresh basil leaves, chopped
> 2 tablespoons fresh oregano, stemmed and chopped
> 2 tablespoons fresh thyme, stemmed and chopped
> 4 pounds Amish Paste Tomatoes, peeled, seeded and diced (8 or 10
>   4 inch-wide tomatoes)

2 medium onions, peeled and diced
¼ cup garlic confit (see recipe)
2 tablespoons fresh garlic, sliced paper thin
1 teaspoon red pepper flake
1 bay leaf
1 cup dry red wine
1 tablespoon fennel seed
Salt and fresh cracked black pepper to taste

Mix the chopped parsley, rosemary, basil, oregano and thyme in a small bowl and set aside.

In a large stock pot, combine the tomatoes, onion, garlic confit, sliced garlic, red pepper flake, bay leaf and red wine. Place this mixture over medium-high heat and bring to a simmer, stirring frequently.

Meanwhile, toast the fennel seeds in a dry sauté pan over medium heat, shaking frequently, until they begin to pop and smoke. Carry the pan around your home to distribute the wonderful aroma. Allow the seeds to cool somewhat, then grind them in a mortar and pestle or spice grinder (same as an electric coffee grinder) to a powder. Add to the tomato mixture, along with half of the mixed herbs.

Allow the sauce to simmer gently, uncovered, for at least 2 hours, or to desired consistency. Stir frequently and adjust heat as necessary to avoid scorching. Taste and adjust with salt and black pepper.

If you are serving it immediately, use the remaining mixed herb to garnish the sauce. If you are cooling and storing it for later use, mix the remaining herbs in after the sauce has cooled. Fresh herbs and cooked herbs offer different flavors, and for this sauce, you want them both.

Yields roughly 3 quarts, depending on how far you choose to cook it down. If you cook it too far for your taste, add some water or wine and readjust the salt.

Out Standing in Their Fields

How Practical Farmers of Iowa Supports Sustainable Farming.

AMES, IA – In 1985 the brief agricultural boom - which had resulted from lowered trade barriers and record Soviet grain purchases - was going bust. The Heartland was in the midst of a crisis it had not seen since the 1930s. Thousands of family farms were lost to overextended loans and collapsing land values. The ecological results of "input intensive" chemical farming were beginning to become clear due to the erosion of topsoil and chemical runoff into rivers and streams. Plummeting commodity prices forced farmers to question economic sustainability of what had become the standard methods of agriculture.

Farming needed a new paradigm. Farmers needed to find practical methods for sustaining their families and their way of life. It was at this time and in this climate that Practical Farmers of Iowa (PFI) was born. Founded as a community based organization by and for producers to share ideas, PFI has grown into an acknowledged leader in science-based research and development of sustainable agriculture practices and new marketing relationships. They have connected time-tested traditions with innovative techniques to create a new and effective way to farm.

PFI's mission is to "research, develop and promote profitable, ecologically sound and community-enhancing approaches to agriculture." Sounds simple enough, but trying to get a roomful of stubborn Iowa farmers to agree on just about anything can be difficult. Using science to help decide what is actually "profitable, ecologically sound, and good for people and communities" is a practical way to avoid any controversies. PFI's research provides concrete proof that certain methods do (or don't) work.

One useful tool for accomplishing this mission is PFI's Farming Systems Program. Through this, farmers learn how to conduct their own on-farm research, with repeated, randomized, results-based testing. For example, in 2005 Rick Exner of Iowa State University and PFI's

Farming Systems Coordinator, organized a study of on-farm flax performance. Another in 2004 addressed hog farmers record keeping and the simple but vital question asked in the name of the study, "Am I Making Money?" The long-range goal of these programs is to not only help the farmers directly, but to move the focus of universities, and of the agribusiness models they support, toward sustainability.

In addition, PFI conducts a Food Systems Program designed to draw closer connections between the farmers and their communities while creating a more equitable and diverse food system. Through an ongoing series of projects, PFI has helped to create new markets for Iowa chestnut growers, taught Community Supported Agriculture organizations about how to market meat, helped farmers learn how to market their products to local restaurants and stores, and done marketing studies on pasture-raised livestock, to cite just a few.

In a joint venture with a national program, PFI is spearheading the "Buy Fresh—Buy Local!" campaign in Iowa. This popular consumer outreach and education program helps food shoppers find and identify food that was grown in their local foodshed, once again drawing closer connections between the community and the farms.

PFI even conducts a Farm Camp for Iowa youth, arranges farm apprenticeships, and works with teachers to create sustainable agriculture curricula. These programs help with a vital issue the whole state is wrestling with: what many have come to call "brain drain." While Iowa offers a comfortable standard of living, a relatively stable economy, and a world-class educational system, the youth of Iowa take that education and beat a path to the hip and trendy urban centers of the country. According to research done by the Leopold Center for Sustainable Agriculture at Iowa State University, the average age of an Iowa farmer in 2005 was 54 and going up. If youth can be shown that farming has a viable future, that it can be a rewarding pursuit, they will be more inclined to stay and carry on the tradition of the family farm.

From Field Days, where members gather at member farms to learn specific techniques, to the Iowa Writers' Circle for those who wish to spread the gospel of sustainability through the written word, PFI is constantly on the cutting edge of innovation in sustainable, practical agriculture.

It is precisely that kind of practical knowledge of the land that PFI is connecting to the modern world: a "third way" where farmers can maintain the tradition of the family farm and still feed their families, where tradition and technology can work together to support the soil rather than erode a way of life.

Iowa Sweet Corn Pancakes

OK, it's true: we have a lot of corn in Iowa. Sadly more and more of it is feed (or fuel) instead of food, but there are still plenty of sources for eye-poppingly wonderful sweet corn. Of course it is marvelous just boiled or grilled and eaten right off the cob, but why not find a more unusual use for it?

These cakes are delicious on their own or paired with any topping your imagination creates – salsas, sautéed mushrooms, smoked trout, barbecued pork – if it sounds like it would be good, then it will.

The corncobs make a delicious stock for soups like corn chowder, or alternatively, dogs love them!

Chiffonade, used here for the basil, is a cutting technique. The word means "ribbon," and refers to the resulting shape and size. Stack the basil leaves on top of the other, then roll them together tightly. Starting at one end of the roll and using a sharp knife, slice the roll as thinly as you can The resulting threads are basil chiffonade. They look nice in any recipe that calls for basil, and the technique works with any leafy herb or vegetable.

- 2 pounds corn on the cob (usually 3-4 ears)
- 2 eggs, beaten
- 1 tablespoons cornstarch
- 2 tablespoons basil, chiffonade
- 1 tablespoon garlic, minced
- 1/4 teaspoon cracked black pepper (or to taste)
- 1 teaspoon salt
- 2 jalapenos, minced (optional)
- 2 tablespoon olive oil

With a sharp knife, slice the corn from the cobs. Set aside half the corn, and place the rest of the ingredients (except the oil) in a food processor. Puree until smooth. Fold in remaining corn.

Heat a nonstick griddle or frying pan over medium-high heat with the olive oil and add dollops of the pancake batter, (roughly 2-3 tablespoons, according to the size you prefer). Cook on one side until bubbles form on top and holes begin to appear, then turn with a spatula and cook through until golden brown on both sides. Serve hot with appropriate sauces and garnishes. Makes 8-12 pancakes, depending on size.

Speaking Truth and Passion

Lynne Rossetto Kasper and a Decade of *The Splendid Table.*

St. Paul, MN – "I wanted to do something where I knew I would never know it all," she said, when asked what interested her in a career in food. Today some might wonder whether she's actually achieved that goal, considering her position as radio's foremost authority on food selection and preparation. She has won a torrent of awards and accolades from every corner of the American food world for both her books and her radio show. Still, after more than twenty years of writing and teaching, and ten years of broadcasting *The Splendid Table* on American Public Media, Lynne Rossetto Kasper is just getting warmed up.

The warm and inviting voice that public radio listeners in over 190 markets across the nation tune in to hear every week, slightly tinged with an accent born in northern New Jersey, is broadcast from the studios of Minnesota Public Radio in St. Paul. Before that, though, there was a career spent traveling the world passionately pursuing knowledge about food.

A background in art and theater helped Kasper land a job in the Abraham and Strauss Department Store in Brooklyn, New York, teaching cooking classes. Some vocational training, as well as time spent cooking her way through Auguste Escoffier's *Le Guide Culinaire* cover to cover, launched her quest for great flavors, and the Strauss job showed her a love for teaching.

She married Frank Kasper and it was often his engineering career that took her to new places. When the couple later moved to Denver, Colorado, Lynne opened a cooking school and began writing articles for magazines. It was during this time she cultivated an interest in local food sources, not only because it was fresher and better tasting, but also because it was easier to get, for example, whole lambs for a butchering demonstration.

A move to Brussels proved to be a watershed moment for Kasper. She continued writing and teaching classes (albeit illegal, clandestine classes in her home to fellow expatriates). From

Brussels, though, one can be in Paris in a couple hours, and Lynne often was. Italy, too, was a frequent host of the eager student and teacher, and would soon prove to be the inspiration for a landmark in the world of American cookbooks—*The Splendid Table: Recipes from Emilia-Romagna, the Heartland of Northern Italian Food.* That, by the way, is a somewhat understated title. Besides being the "Heartland of Northern Italian Food," Emilia-Romagna is indeed the culinary epicenter of the western world (not, as some would have you believe, Paris or Lyon).

Reluctantly, the couple returned to the U.S. in 1985, this time to the Twin Cities, and *The Splendid Table* was published in 1992. This is when that torrent of awards that I mentioned began. The International Association of Culinary Professionals gave its Julia Child Award for the best cookbook by a first-time author, and awarded her book Cookbook of the Year. The James Beard Award for Cookbook of the Year soon followed. *Splendid Table* is the first and only book to have garnered all three crowns, and Lynne was an instant celebrity in the food world.

In 1995, a radio producer named Sally Swift suggested an idea for a show, and wanted Lynne to host. Minnesota Public Radio backed the idea right away, and it wasn't long before the show, named for that first book, was syndicated. Over the decade since, Lynne and Sally have built one of the most popular call-in programs on the air, receiving more James Beard awards for best show, best host and "one of the 12 best cooking teachers in America." All this is in addition to the high honor of being lampooned on *Saturday Night Live,* a tribute given to only one other culinary icon, none other than Julia Child.

A long time Slow Food member, Lynne is always talking on the show about the same values Slow Food espouses, those of tradition, authenticity, seasonality and placeness. Every once in a while, though, she actually addresses the movement more directly, like the show in 2003 when she toured Manhattan's Lower East Side with Ben Watson, coauthor of *The Slow Food Guide to New York Restaurants, Markets and Bars.* From the Doughnut Plant on Grand Street, up the street to Kosar's Bialys; from Russ and Daughter's Appetizers on Houston for smoked fish to Il Laboratorio del Gelato for dessert.

The subject of gelato, that luscious Italian Ice Cream, came up during my visit with Lynne, so she took me to Café Crema in Minneapolis for espresso and some samples of their amazing gelatos. Not only were the traditional flavors marvelous, but we were both intrigued by more experimental flavors such as "olive oil and *fleur de sel*." Fleur de sel is a kind of sea salt, harvested from the reeds on seacoasts from Brittany to Marseilles. I know it sounds a little strange, a gelato with oil and salt, but it was quite delicious, and we agreed it would be a delightful garnish on a chilled tomato bisque.

What has a decade of hosting *The Splendid Table* taught her? "Great teachers make the best interviews," she said, as she sipped her cappuccino, This reminded her of the example of professor Sidney Perkowitz, whom she interviewed years ago, about his book *Universal Foam: from Cappuccino to the Cosmos*. Perkowitz is a physicist who explains the structure of foams in a very approachable way, and he shared a unique view on how to make great culinary foams. Not the curious, contrived creations of Spanish star chef Ferran Adria, but the classic foams that make up bread, beer and soufflés.

Lynne's fondness for interviewing teachers is an understandable one, because she is still a teacher herself at heart, still sharing her passion for amazing flavors and culinary traditions. Through *The Splendid Table*, Lynne Rossetto Kasper is able to help people all over the country understand that cooking is not a chore to be avoided but a unique pleasure to be pursued with love and passion and friends and family.

Sweet Rosemary-Pear Pizza

When Lynne Rossetto Kasper was a guest at the Field to Family Festival of Local Foods in Iowa City in 2002, she demonstrated the preparation of this dish for the crowd at the Iowa City Farmers' Market. Her book *The Italian Country Table* had just been released, and it included this recipe. It is used here with the author's permission.

Dishes like this one are a great way to get finicky kids to broaden their palates a little bit. I've never met a kid who didn't like it.

  1 ½ cups unbleached flour, preferably organic
  Generous ¼ teaspoon salt
  1 ½ teaspoons sugar
  ½ cup cold unsalted butter, cut into chunks
  1 large egg, beaten
  2 to 3 tablespoons cold water

  4 firm-ripe Bosc pears, preferably organic (1 ½ to 2 pounds)
  ½ lemon
  shredded zest of 1 large orange
  1 tablespoon fresh basil leaves, chopped
  1 teaspoon fresh rosemary, finely chopped
  1 teaspoon ground cinnamon
  ¼ teaspoon freshly ground black pepper
  ½ cup sugar
  2 tablespoons extra-virgin olive oil

Combine dry pastry ingredients - flour, salt, and sugar - in food processor or large bowl. Cut in butter with rapid pulses in processor, or rub between fingertips until dough breaks into pea-size shapes. Add egg and 2 tablespoons of the water. Pulse just until dough gathers in clumps, or toss with fork until evenly moistened. If dough seems dry, blend in another ½ to 1 tablespoon of water. Lightly brush a little olive oil on a 14- to 16-inch pizza pan.

Roll out dough on floured board to an extremely thin 17-inch round. Place on pan. Don't trim excess pastry; loosely fold it over toward center of pie. Refrigerate 30 minutes to overnight.

Set oven rack on lowest position and preheat oven to 500° Take dough out of refrigerator. Peel, core, halve, and stem pears. Slice vertically into half-inch-wide wedges, about 14 slices per pear. Moisten with a little lemon juice. Fold back dough's rim so it hangs over edge of pan.

Arrange pear slices in overlapping spiral on dough, starting right at rim of pan. Sprinkle with orange zest, basil, rosemary, cinnamon, pepper, sugar, and oil. Flip overhanging crust onto pears.

Bake until pears are speckled golden brown and crust is crisp, 15 to 20 minutes. Cover crust's rim with foil if it browns too quickly. Remove pizza from oven and serve hot, warm, or at room temperature. Makes 8 to 10 servings.

Farm to Kitchen to Table
The Scattergood Method of Creating Citizens.

WEST BRANCH, IA - Imagine a school where the students take an active role in the production of their own food, from plant to plate. They till the soil, sow the seeds, pull the weeds, harvest, cook and enjoy the food. They compost the scrap. Students even feed cows, chickens, sheep and pigs; all this while receiving a first-class, college-prep education.

That's not all. In an atmosphere that emphasizes personal responsibility as well as community cooperation, these high school students clean the classrooms, the bathrooms, the cafeteria and more. One week they are building a new classroom, the next they are sweeping the library, all this right alongside the faculty, who participate in these work crews too.

Students learn all the basics you would expect a school to teach: advanced math, English, foreign language, history, humanities, research and composition. They also learn pottery, even glass blowing and fencing.

Lest you think this is some hippie commune, you should know that each student carries a notebook computer with school-wide WiFi internet access (students help maintain the network, too).

Sound like a fancy east coast private school? It's right down the road from Iowa City, Iowa, in West Branch. Is this a new idea? It was founded in 1890 by the Religious Society of Friends (the Quakers). Sound impossible? Sound like a pipe dream? It's not. It's Scattergood.

The goal of Scattergood is to prepare students for college and for life by instilling them with recognition of self-worth, a sense of global citizenship, growing spiritual awareness, a commitment to lifelong learning, the ability to live constructively in a community, and the skills to attain future academic and vocational success. It's hard not to love a school that can do all that. Of course, it is Scattergood's philosophy of food that has me waxing philosophic.

Students and teachers work together to plant, grow, harvest, and cook the food in a convivial form of cooperation that can only lead to enlightened learning.

Scattergood believes that all work has dignity and is intrinsically rewarding, which happens to jibe perfectly with what I've been saying in these pages: that cooking is not a hassle to be performed grudgingly. Rather, it is a sincere act of faith and love that should be performed with a certain reverence. Students at Scattergood learn the importance of this ritual from day one.

The eighty-acre farm is run with a three-pronged approach. It is a "living laboratory" where nearly any subject can be taught. Biology to be sure, but also math, physics, history, sexuality - name a subject, it can be taught in the three-acre organic garden. The farm is also an economic enterprise, not only feeding the campus but also selling produce to the New Pioneer Co-op in Iowa City and to individuals through Scattergood's own Community Supported Agriculture (CSA) program - all this while teaching the students useful farm skills.

Among the many positive results of this: a 100% (that's not a typo) college placement record. In fact, acceptance to college is a requirement for graduation.

The food is never fancy, but it is always homemade, always nutritious, and made by people who care about the quality because they are making it for themselves. Scattergood Art Projects instructor and chef-in-residence, Dana Foster, has been with the school since 1993. She said, "By working in a from-scratch kitchen, students learn that food doesn't come from a mix or a freezer box. It doesn't even have to come from the grocery store!" Meals can be as simple as red beans and rice or as elaborate as a whole lamb spit-roasted over glowing oak embers. Every ingredient feasible comes from the Scattergood farm.

The farm in turn serves as an outdoor classroom and laboratory, where students can work on projects ranging from orchard care to raising heritage breed chickens to all-night vigils during lambing season. Humanities instructor and farm manager, Mark Quee, who came to Scattergood in 1999, loves his work at the school because it allows him to "nurture [his] many selves: teacher, lover of books and films, outdoors explorer, organic farmer and one who appreciates living in community."

Scattergood Friends School offers students an environment where every moment is a teachable one, and where learning encompasses the whole world.

Gingered Cucumbers

The students at Scattergood tend to a three-acre organic plot that turns out all sorts of delicious produce for the students and for the CSA that the school operates for local families. One of my favorite summer treats is the cucumbers, and this is a simple, Southeast-Asian style salad that can preserve the abundance of any summer garden.

The serrano peppers are optional, but if you do use them, use caution. They are fierce, and just a little near your eyes or nose can cause real pain. Wear gloves and/or wash your hands well after handling.

  2 cups white vinegar
  1 cup water
  1/4 cup soy sauce
  4 tablespoons fresh grated ginger
  2 tablespoons sugar or honey (or to taste)
  8 cucumbers
  2 carrots, shredded
  1 bunch scallions (about 10), bias-sliced thin
  1/2 cup fresh cilantro, chopped
  2 serrano peppers, minced (or to taste)
  Salt and white pepper to taste
  1/2 cup roasted peanuts, chopped (optional garnish)

Mix the liquid ingredients with the ginger and sugar (or honey), stir until sugar is dissolved, and set aside.

If your cucumbers are the standard store-bought kind that are dipped in wax, the should be peeled. Otherwise simply wash them thoroughly and slice them in half lengthwise. Using a teaspoon, gently scoop out the seeds and either save them for next year or compost them. Slice the cucumbers on a bias, as thin as possible.

Toss with the carrots, scallions, cilantro and peppers (if desired). Add the vinegar mixture and mix thoroughly. Taste and adjust with salt and white pepper. Refrigerate two hours to overnight.

Serve garnished with the peanuts and/or a cilantro sprig.

This salad will keep almost indefinitely in the refrigerator because it is, essentially, a pickle.

Putting Beliefs to Work

Robert Waldrop, and the Oklahoma Food Cooperative.

Oklahoma City, OK – As with most Midwestern states, folks who are unfamiliar with Oklahoma have some well-established notions about what it looks like and who lives there. Mostly, these ideas come from grim, Dust Bowl era black and white photographs and cable TV reruns of the old Rogers and Hammerstein musical. Beyond that, Oklahoma is known to outsiders for top-tier football, particularly nasty tornadoes, and wildcatting oil prospectors. Of course, all of America now quickly thinks of the tragedy of the terrorist bombing of the Murrow Federal Building whenever Oklahoma City is mentioned.

What is not often mentioned, when you ask someone for his or her thoughts on Oklahoma, is the food. Few non-Sooners are aware of the history and culture that surround the food and agriculture of today's Oklahoma. Even many residents of the state, subject to the standardization of flavors offered by fast food restaurants, are unaware that the best food in Oklahoma comes from right there in their home state rather than out of a freezer bag, or at the local burger joint.

Robert Waldrop is on a campaign to change all that. The Oklahoma Food Cooperative, which Robert founded in the fall of 2003, began as an index of Oklahoma family farms that were producing food for sale directly to the consumer. It has grown into a cooperative with 73 producers and nearly 450 members statewide. It has been a tremendous boon to all involved, the cooperative now acts like a buying club: supplying, ordering, and distributing.

Members, who must be Oklahoma residents, can visit the website at OklahomaFood.org and place their orders from the list of what's in season each month. At any given time, that list might contain organic sourdough bread ($3.99 for a 1.3 pound loaf in 2005) from Springhill Farms in Roosevelt. There, Nick and Karen Callen not only bake wonderful breads from locally grown and milled grains and make a fine salsa (red or green), they also raise cows, goats for meat, and, curiously, guard donkeys.

The cooperative product list might also contain Bolerjack's Bodacious Barbecue Sauce, free-range eggs from Redbird Ranch in Webbers Falls, herbs from Kygar Road Greenhouse in Ponca City, bison T-bone steak from James Stepp's Wichita Buffalo Company in Hinton, and fallow deer from Jerry and JoAnn Logan at Honey Hill Farm in Guthrie (see the chapter on them in this book). Different seasons bring different products to the table, but the list is always extensive, and everything is Oklahoma-made.

Born of Robert's dedicated involvement with the Catholic Worker Movement and its Oscar Romero House in Oklahoma City, the cooperative strives not only to provide delicious food to Oklahomans but also to teach and spread the gospel of sustainability in all aspects of life. The connection between the religious workers' support network, founded in New York in 1933, and sustainable agriculture in Oklahoma may not be immediately apparent, but to Waldrop, every aspect of life is intertwined with every other. He points out that the movement's founder, Dorothy Day, said that their purpose was "to make it easier for people to be good." To Waldrop, providing fresh, healthful food, and helping to see that more Oklahoman money stays in Oklahoma, is a great way to do just that.

His work and his beliefs come together in serendipitous ways. I had the pleasure of meeting Robert in Oklahoma City in 2003, and I helped him serve dinner in a church basement to bus loads of workers from Immokalee, Florida. These workers were on the return leg of their journey to Los Angeles to stage a protest at the headquarters of Taco Bell, a subsidiary of Yum! Brands. The Coalition of Immokalee Workers (CIW) was out to persuade Taco Bell to do its part to end the horrendous working conditions of the tomato pickers in Florida. Writing from the Carter Center in Atlanta, former U.S. President Jimmy Carter stated: "I have followed with concern for a number of years the appalling working conditions in the Florida-based tomato industry. While production costs in the industry have increased over the last 25 years, wages have been effectively stagnant, as giant cooperative buying mechanisms hold prices down. Conditions are so bad in parts of the industry that there have been two separate prosecutions for slavery in recent years." The CIW exists in part to persuade "Yum! Brands" and Taco Bell to play their part in pulling these farms out of the 19th century. Miraculously, in March of 2005, Yum! Brands relented, and agreed to the demands of the CIW. Other large chains have since followed suit, though as of this writing, Burger King remains a hold out.

An important part of what slow food is about is knowing the source of the food, something called traceability. There can be more to this though than simply knowing that my lobster came from Maine, my potato from Idaho or my tomato from Florida. An awareness of the people involved is vital. It lends a spiritual layer to the consumption of the food that is beyond description when the grower is my friend. When the grower is mistreated or worse and I buy that product, well, that's too bitter a taste for me to swallow.

Waldrop's meal for the exhausted Immokalee protestors, of macaroni in a homemade sauce of local tomatoes and Oklahoma bison, was not fancy, but it was definitely slow food. Belief in these ideas led Robert to be a delegate to Terra Madre in 2004, and led him to create the Food Co-op which is helping people across the state of Oklahoma by connecting farmers with consumers, all of whom care about the land and their food.

Oklahoma City Chili

1 1/2 pounds lean ground beef or bison
1 Tablespoon olive oil
2 medium onions, diced
4 cloves garlic, minced
3/4 Teaspoon salt
1 teaspoon fresh-cracked black pepper
1 medium green bell pepper diced
1 medium red bell pepper diced
1 cup corn kernels (frozen is fine)
4 Tablespoons (or to taste) hot smoked Spanish paprika
2 hot peppers of your choice, seeded and minced
1/2 pound (dry weight) cooked pinto beans
1 15 ounce can diced tomatoes
1 15 ounce can tomato puree
12 ounces dark beer (such as bock)
4 Tablespoons toasted cumin seed, ground
1 Tablespoon Worcestershire sauce

In a large stockpot, cook ground beef in olive oil over medium-high heat with onion, garlic, salt and pepper until browned well. Break up meat with a spoon as you cook. Add bell peppers, corn, and hot peppers. Continue to cook on low heat until peppers are tender, about five minutes. Stir occasionally.

Add the remaining ingredients and gently bring to a simmer. Allow to simmer for 2-3 hours, then turn off heat and allow to cool. Reheat when ready to eat. Serve with grated cheese, chopped onions, cornbread, tortilla chips or any of the thousands of accompaniments you wish.

The Seed of the Great Spirit

Winona LaDuke and the White Earth Land Recovery Project.

PONSFORD, MN – Hidden way back in the North Woods, well off the paved roads, on the White Earth Reservation is the home of Winona LaDuke. From her ancestral land she is leading a quiet revolution to save a way of life.

Though Winona was not born on this land, her father was a member of the Makwa Dodaem, or Bear Clan, of the Mississippi band of the Anishinaabe, or Ojibwe tribe on the White Earth Reservation. Her mother was the daughter of Polish immigrants, and Winona was born in California, where her father worked as an actor in Western movies.

Her activism in Native American Rights began while she was attending Harvard, and her star rose quickly – she was speaking on the subject before the United Nations at age 18. By 2000 she was running for Vice President of the United States on the Green Party ticket.

Back in 1867 the US Federal Government designated 1300 square miles of territory in Northern Minnesota as the White Earth Reservation, setting aside this land for the Anishinaabeg (Ojibwe) people. One hundred years later less than ten percent of the original 837,000 acres of land was in native hands, having been taken away by land developers or confiscated in tax debt repayment. In 1989 LaDuke founded The White Earth Land Recovery Project (WELRP) to get that land back. To date they have placed more than 1700 acres of community land in trust for the Ojibwe people, but that is just the beginning. At this writing they are looking to purchase six acres for a food production facility, and looking into additional land for wind turbine electrical production.

This land is sacred to the Ojibwe people because of their ancient spiritual connection to it through the food it provides, which comes from their migration stories in which the Ojibwe were told by the Creator to go to the place where the Manoomin (which translates roughly to "good berry") grows on the water. They found that place in the Northern Great Lakes region and lived healthy lives for centuries harvesting the Creator's gift to the people, wild rice.

Though the English term for Manoomin is wild rice, it is actually not rice (*Oryza sativa*) but rather the seed of an aquatic grass (*Zizania palustris*) and is related to corn. It has far more protein than rice, which is why it sustains health so well.

Until the 1960's the Anishinaabe had a virtual monopoly on wild rice production, but that changed when the University of Minnesota figured out a way to cultivate it. In 1977 the Law of Unintended Consequences kicked in when the state legislature declared wild rice the "Official State Grain," a kind gesture that caused massive amounts of research dollars to pour in. The ironically named "cultivated wild rice," or paddy rice, became big industry in one of the United States' biggest grain economies. Prices plummeted, and the natives on the White Earth Reservation and throughout the region could fetch no more than twenty-five cents per pound. For a product that takes days and days of hard physical labor to harvest and parch, such a price was completely debilitating.

WELRP helps native Manoomin harvesters by paying upwards of $1.25 per pound (in 2005) for their hand harvested rice. They parch it in large batches with that of other tribal members and create markets where it can fetch a fair price. In 2000, Winona and WELRP were honored with the Slow Food Award for Biodiversity. LaDuke says it expanded their thinking. "We didn't know we were Slow Food people," she said. So many are and don't know it.

Additionally, Slow Food began the very first American Presidium in defense of hand harvested, hand parched Native American Wild Rice. The purpose of all the Slow Food Presidia is to promote artisan products; to stabilize production techniques; to establish stringent production standards and, above all, to guarantee a viable future for traditional foods (so that we can continue to enjoy them). Slow Food works with the producers to create viable markets for their product because if a traditional artisanal food can have an economic impact, it can be brought back from the verge of extinction.

This association has broadened their thinking on the White Earth Reservation as well. Now there are Ojibwe farmers raising the Heritage Turkey breeds, and people all over the country and the world recognizing the flavor and importance of real Manoomin.

Today Manoomin faces additional challenges. Researchers at the Department of Agronomy and Plant Genetics at the University of Minnesota are mapping the genome of wild rice. This is the initial step to the genetic manipulation (GM) of the food and to the patenting of laboratory-created, "improved" strains of rice. The long- and short-term implications of this to the health of the environment, to the Ojibwe people, and to consumers are completely unknown.

Of course the Ojibwe have banned GM crops from their land, but that does not mean they won't get there. Pollen carried on the wind or seed blowing off passing trucks is more than enough to cause damage. If the DNA of some future, GM wild rice shows up in the lakes of the White Earth Reservation, it could have effects on all the rice on Native land.

LaDuke's vigilance is stemming the tide in the Ojibwe's scenic corner of the world, but much more work must be done. In 2004, she joined with 5000 other artisans, farmers, and food producers from 120 nations in Torino, Italy, for an event called Terra Madre: A World Gathering of Food Communities. Terra Madre 2004 was an effort to build a global network of people who were concerned with the long-term viability of their ways of life. An enormous success, Terra Madre has become a biennial event, "attentive to environmental resources, planetary balance, the quality of the finished product, the dignity of workers and the health of consumers, (Terra Madre) will unite producers and farmers from all over the world who together represent a different and more complex way of understanding the food system."

Most stories such as Winona LaDuke's could get lost in the background noise of the information age, but her relentless pursuit of what is rightfully hers, rightfully the spirit of the Ojibwe people, will not be silenced.

Wild Rice Dressing

For as long as I can remember, this dish has been the indicative flavor and aroma of Thanksgiving, which is my favorite holiday. It's the one day in America where everybody really concentrates on being around a table with great food and the people they love.

Winona told me that it's important to remember, when using the hand-parched, truly wild rice, that it cooks much faster than the cultivated "paddy rice." The running joke on the White Earth Reservation goes "How to cook Paddy Rice: Put rice and water in a pot with a stone and boil. When the stone is soft, the rice is almost done."

    1 pound hand-parched, Manoomin wild rice, washed
    3 cups chicken stock
    1 pound "breakfast-style" sage pork sausage
    ¼ pound butter
    2 portobello mushrooms, diced
    ½ onion, minced
    1 tablespoon parsley, chopped
    1 stalk celery, diced
    1 tablespoon fresh sage, chopped
    1 pinch fresh thyme
    Salt and white pepper to taste

Preheat oven to 350°

Rinse rice thoroughly in 3 changes of hot tap water. Put rice and stock in a large pot and bring to a boil. Boil rice in broth for 20 minutes, or until all the liquid is absorbed.

Meanwhile, brown sausage in butter until fully cooked. Add remaining ingredients. Simmer 10 minutes. Mix in the rice. Transfer to a covered casserole. Bake covered at 350° for 20 minutes, then uncovered to desired consistency – I like it a little crunchy on top.

Serves 4-6 as a side dish.

APPENDICES

CERTIFIED ORGANIC
GARLIC SCAPES
$2.00/BUNCH
WE HAVE RECIPE SHEETS!

Contacts and Resources by State

By no means comprehensive, here are just a few of the wonderful people and places throughout the Heartland that, one way or another, support some or all of the ideals of living the Slow Food way. One may appreciate the amazing depths of a long hardwood smoke; another may buy everything locally and/or organically; still another may be raising Slow Food USA Ark – Registered foods. A deep and abiding love of food is shared by all who are listed here.

No book can always be entirely up-to-date, so always call ahead or write before visiting.

Finally, at the end of this appendix is a listing of a few additional Slow Food resources throughout the nation and the world.

Illinois

Angelic Organics CSA Learning Center
Tom Spaulding
1547 Rockton Road
Caledonia, IL   61011
815.389.8455
www.LearnGrowConnect.org

Paul and Joey Bane
Slow Food Ark USA Registered Heritage Turkeys
1062 County Road, 2125 E
Sidney, IL 61877
217.688.2447
www.TomMccowan.com

Caveny Farm
Slow Food Ark USA-Registered Heritage Turkeys
John Caveny
1999 N. 935 E. Road
Monticello, IL 61856
217-762-7767
www.CavenryFarm.com

Goose Island Brewery
1800 N Clybourn Avenue
Chicago, IL 60614
312.915.0071
www.GooseIsland.com

Heartland Meats
Piedmontese Beef
Pat and John Sondgeroth
204 E US Route 52
Mendota, IL 61342
877.588.5326
www.HeartlandMeats.com

Henry's Farm
Henry and Hiroko Brockman
"More-ganic Family Farm"
432 Grimm Road
Congerville, IL 61729
www.HenrysFarm.com

Herbally Yours, Artisanal vinegars, oils, and mustards
Jim and Kathy Vitalo
409 Forest Avenue
Willow Springs, IL 60480-1421
708.839.8969
www.HerballyYours.bravehost.com

Intelligentsia Coffee Roasters
1850 W. Fulton
Chicago, IL 60612
312.563.0023
www.IntelligentsiaCoffee.com

The Land Connection
Terra Brockman, Director
1569 Sugar Hill Lane
Congerville, IL 61729
309.678.2672
www.TheLandConnection.org

Kinnikinnick Farms, Organic produce
David and Susan Cleverdon
21123 Grade School Road
Caledonia, Il 61011
815.292.3288

Mulberry Lane Farm,
Organic produce, goats, turkeys, chickens
Helen Aardsma
414 N. Mulberry
Loda, IL 60948

Organic Pastures
Larry and Marilyn Wettstein
169 Ct. Rd 1800 E
Eureka, IL 61530
orgpas@mtco.com

Prairie Fruits Farm
Goat Cheeses, Leslie Cooperband
4410 N. Lincoln Avenue
Champaign, IL 61822-9455
217.643.2314
www.PrairieFruits.com

Purple Asparagus
Educational organization dedicated to
bringing families back to the table
Melissa Graham
1824 W. Newport Avenue
Chicago, IL 60657
773.991.1920
www.PurpleAsparagus.com

Wettstein Organic Farm
2100 US Highway 150
Carlock, Illinois 761725
309.376.7291

Restaurants and Markets—Illinois

17th Street Bar and Grill
Pitmaster Mike Mills
32 N. 17th Street
Murphysboro, IL 62966
618.684.3722 or 618.684.8902
www.17thStreetBarbeques.com

Bistro Campagne
Chef Michael Altenberg
4518 N. Lincoln Avenue
Chicago, IL 60625
773.271.6100
www.BistroCampagne.com

Blackbird
Chef Paul Kahan
619 W Randolph St
Chicago, IL 60606
312.715.0708
www.BlackbirdRestaurant.com

Campagnola
Chef Michael Altenberg
815 Chicago Avenue
Evanston, IL 60202-2307
847.475.6100
www.CampagnolaRestaurant.com

Green City Market, Lincoln park
www.ChicagoGreenCityMarket.org

Green Zebra
1460 W Chicago Avenue
Chicago, IL 60622
312.243.7100
www.GreenZebraChicago.com

Erwin
Erwin and Cathy Drechsler
2925 N. Halsted Street
Chicago, IL 60657
773-528-7200
www.ErwinCafe.com

Frontera Grill and Topolobambo
Chef Rick Bayless
445 N. Clark,
Chicago, IL 60610
312.661.1434
www.FronteraKitchens.com

Lula Café
Amalea Tshilds and Jason Hammel
2537 North Kedzie Blvd
Chicago, IL 60647
www.LulaCafe.com

Mas
Chef John Manion
1670 West Division
Chicago, IL 60622
773.276.8700
www.MasRestaurant.com

North Pond
Chef Bruce Sherman
2610 N Cannon Dr.
Chicago, IL 60614
773.477.5845
www.NorthPondRestaurant.com

La Petite Folie
Mary and Michael Mastricola
1504 East 55th Street
Chicago, IL 60615
773.493.1394
www.LaPetiteFolie.com

TAC Thai Quick Kitchen
3930 N. Sheridan
Chicago, IL 60613
773.327.5253

Thyme
Chef John Bubala
464 N. Halsted
Chicago, IL 60622
312.226.4300
www.ThymeChicago.com

Vie
Chef Paul Virant
4471 Lawn Ave
Western Springs, IL 60558
708.246.2082
www.VieRestaurant.com

Indiana

Apple Family Farm
Debbie Apple (co-director of Slow Food Indy)
7806 N. 300 W
McCordsville, IN 46055-9690
www.AppleFamilyFarm.com

Capriole Goat Cheese
Judith Shad
P.O.Box 117
10329 Newcut Road
Greenville, IN 47124
812.923.9408
www.CaprioleGoatCheese.com

Doud's County Line Orchards
Apples, peaches, pears
David Doud
7877 West 400 N.
Wabash, IN 46992
765.833.6122

Double T Ranch
Farm-raised venison
Tim Tague
2913 Hollow Branch Trail
Martinsville, IN 46151
888.349.1889
www.VensionDeerFarmer.com

Great Circle Farm CSA
Beth Neff
201 N. 22nd St
Goshen, IN 46525
219.533.7936

Harvest Moon Flower Farm
Linda Chapman and Daryl Dale
3592 Harvest Moon Ln.
Spencer, IN 47460
812.829.3517
www.HarvestMoonFlowerFarm.com

Heartland Family Farm
Teresa Birtles
1949 Sunny Acres Dr
Bedford, IN 47421
812.279.0480

Hickoryworks
Shagbark hickory syrup
Gordon and Sherry Jones
3615 Peoga Rd
Trafalgar, IN 46181
317.878.5648
www.Hickoryworks.com

Hoosier Organic Marketing Education, Inc.
8364 S. S.R. 39
Clayton, IN 46118
765.539.6935

Indiana Sustainable Agriculture Association
Steve Bonney
100 Georgeton Ct
West Lafayette, IN 47906
765.463.9366
sbonney@iquest.net

Meadowlark Organic Farm
Marcia Veldman
6181 Kent Rd
Bloomington, IN 47401
812.988.4956

Natural Bounty Greenhouse and Farm
David and Sara Ring
12660 E. Eaton-Albany Pike
Dunkirk, IN 47336
765.789.4489
www.RingFamilyFarm.com

New Day Meadery
Brett Canaday and Tia Agnew
701 South Anderson St.
Elwood, IN 46036
765.552.3433
www.NewDayMeadery.com

Poe Stock Farm
Stanley Poe
2213 W State Rd. 144
Franklin, IN 46131
317.738.0863

Trader's Point Organic Dairy and Farmers' Market
David Robb
9101 Moore Road
Zionsville, IN 46077
317.733.1700
www.TPFOrganics.com

The Swiss Connection
Ice Cream and Cheese, Beef and Veal
Alan and Kate Yegerlehner
1087 E. County Rd. 550 S
Clay City, IN 47841
812.939.2813

Wib's Stone Ground Grits
Cornmeal, grits, whole wheat flour &
buckwheat flour
Chris Voster
Odon, IN 47562
812.636.8066, 888.349.1889

Your Neighbor's Garden
Variety of Indiana local fruits and vegetables
Ross and Sherry Faris
5224 Grandview Drive
Indianapolis, In
317.251.4130
www.YourNeighborsGarden.com

Restaurants and Markets—Indiana

Citrus at The Checkerberry Inn
Chef Kelly Graf
62644 County Road 37
Goshen, IN 46528
574.642.0191
www.CitrusRestaurant.com

Elements Restaurant
Chef Owner Greg Hardesty
415 N Alabama
Indianapolis, IN 46204
317.634.8888
www.ElementsIndy.com

Limestone Grille
Chef Tad DeLay
2920 East Covenanter Drive
Bloomington, IN 47401
812.335.8110
www.LimestoneGrille.com

H2O Sushi
Chef Owner Greg Hardesty
1912 Broad Ripple Ave
Indianapolis, IN 46220-2328
317.254.0677
www.H2Osushibar.com

Mill Race Center Farmers' Market
Zelda Stoltzfus
212 W. Washington Ave.
Goshen, IN 46526
219.534.4747
www.MillRace.org

Rbistro
Chef Regina Mehallick
888 Massachusetts Ave
Indianapolis, IN 46202
317.423.0312
www.Rbistro.com

Restaurant Tallent
Chef David Tallent
208 N Walnut
Bloomington, IN 47404
812.330.9801
www.RestaurantTallent.com

Iowa

Bochner Chocolates
Eric Bochner
2445 2nd St. Suite 2
Coralville, IA 52241
319.354.7900
www.BochnerChocolates.com

Cleverley Farms CSA
Organic Garlic, Greens, Vegetables
Larry Cleverley
8694 Highway 330 North
Mingo, IA 50168
641.363.4299

Farmers' All-Natural Creamery
1010 540th St SW
Wellman, IA 52356
319.646.2200
www.FarmersAllNaturalCreamery.com

Iowa Network for Community Agriculture
Jan Libbey
1465 120th St
Kanawha, IA 50447
641.495.6367
www.GrowInca.org

Jordan Creek Bison Farm
Bill Leefers, Chief Executive Cogitator
PO Box 517
1873 Jordan Creek Rd
Solon, IA 52333
319.644.3535

Leopold Center for Sustainable Agriculture
Frederick Kirschenmann, Director
209 Curtiss Hall
Iowa State University
Ames, Iowa 50011-1050
515.294.3711
www.leopold.iastate.edu

Local Harvest CSA
Susan Jutz
5025 120th Street NE
Solon, IA 52333
319.624.3052
www.ZJfarms.com

Local Foods Connection
Laura Dowd
PO Box 2821
Iowa City, Iowa 52244
localfoodsconnection@yahoo.com
www.LocalFoodsConnection.org

Midwest Sustainable Agriculture Working Group
Teresa Opheim, Coordinator
1614 Morningside Dr
Iowa City, IA 52245
319.354.0258
www.msawg.org

Millstream Brewing
Brewmaster Aaron Taubman
PO Box 284
835 48th Ave
Amana, IA 55203
319.622.3672
www.MillstreamBrewing.com

Northern Prairie Chevre
Kathy Larson, Wendy Mickle, Connie Lawrance
1247 310th Street
Woodward, IA 50276
515.438.4022
www.NorthernPrairieChevre.com

Paul's Grains
Wayne, Betty, Steve, and Teresa Paul
2475-B 340th St.
Laurel, IA 50141
641.476.3373
www.PaulsGrains.com

Practical Farmers of Iowa
P.O. Box 349
Ames, Iowa 50010
515.232.5661
www.PracticalFarmers.org

La Quercia Prosciutto
Herb and Kathy Eckhouse
400 Hakes Drive
Norwalk, Iowa 50211
515.981.1625
www.LaQuercia.us

Simone's Plain and Simple
A Member Farm of Local Harvest CSA
Farmhouse Dinners by Appointment
Simone Delaty
1478 470th St.
Wellman, IA 52356
319.683.2896
www.SimonePlainAndSimple.com

Scattergood School Farm
1951 Delta Avenue
West Branch, IA 52358
319.643.7600 or 888.737.4376
www.Scattergood.org

Seed Savers Exchange
Diane Ott Whealy
3094 N Winn Rd
Decorah, IA 52101
563.382.5990
www.SeedSavers.org

Surya Nagar Farm
Lonnie Gamble
1860 Woodland Dr
Fairfield, IA 52556
641.469.5240
www.BigGreenSummer.com

Restaurants and Markets—Iowa

Augusta
101 South Augusta
Oxford, IA 52322
319.828.2252
www.AugustaRestaurant.net

Atlas World Grill
127 Iowa Ave
Iowa City, IA 52240
www.AtlasIowaCity.com

The Café
Kevin Rettig
2616 Northridge Pkwy
Ames, IA 50010
515.292.0100

Devotay
Kim McWane Friese and Chef Kurt Michael Friese
117 North Linn St.
Iowa City, IA 52245
319.354.1001
www.Devotay.net

Azalea Restaurant & Zen Sushi Bar
400 Walnut
Des Moines, Iowa 50309
1.515.288.9606
www.Azaleadsm.com

Haight's Hawkeye Meat Market
100 E Oakdale Blvd # 400
Coralville, IA 52241
319.338.2929
www.HawkeyeMeatMarket.com

The Lincoln Café
Chef Matthew Steigerwald
117 1st Street W
Mt. Vernon, IA 52314
319.895.4041
www.FoodIsImportant.com

The Motley Cow
160 North Linn Street
Iowa City, IA 52245
319.688.9177

New Pioneer Co-op
22 S. Van Buren
Iowa City, IA 52240
319.338.9441
www.NewPi.com

126
126 E Washington St
Iowa City, IA 52240
319.887.1909
www.onetwentysix.net

Phoenix Café and Inn
Kamal Hammouda
834 Park St SE
Grinnell, IA 50112
641.236.3657
www.ThePhoenixCafe.com

the red avocado
521 e. washington st.
iowa city, ia 52240
319.351.6088
www.TheRedAvocado.com

Ruzicka's Meat Locker
301 N Dubuque St
Solon, IA 52333
319.644.2870

Star Bar
2811 Ingersoll Ave
Des Moines, Iowa 50312
1.515.244.0790
www.Starbardsm.com

Kansas

Berning Organic Grains
Jerome Berning
Rt. 1, Box 2E
Marienthal, KS 67863
burnblue@yahoo.com

Freestate Brewing
636 Massachusetts Street
Lawrence, KS 66044
785.843.4555
www.FreestateBrewing.com

Heartland Sustainable Agriculture Network
Jerry Jost
2002 E. 1600 Road
Lawrence, KS 66044
913.841.7044
jjost@kansasruralcenter.org

Jako, Inc.
Dairy Products, Poultry, Pigs & Lamb
6003 E Eales Rd
Hutchinson, KS 67501
877.525.6462
www.JakoInc.com

Kansas Center for Sustainable Agriculture
and Alternative Crops
Jana Beckman, Coordinator
3029 Throckmorton Hall
Manhattan, Ks 66506
785.532.1440
www.KansasSustainableAg.org

Kansas City Center for Urban Agriculture and
the Kansas City Community Farm
Katherine Kelly
PO Box 6043
Kansas City, KS 66106
913.831.2444
www.Kccua.org

Louisburg Cider Mill
Shelly and Tom Schierman
14730 Hwy 68
Louisburg, KS, 66053
800.748.7765
www.LouisburgCiderMill.com

Mother Earth News
Bryan Welch, Publisher
Ogden Publications, Inc.,
1503 SW 42nd St.
Topeka, Kansas 66609-1265
www.MotherEarthNews.com

Somerset Ridge Winery
Dennis and Cindy Reynolds, Proprietors
29725 Somerset Road
Somerset, KS 66071
913.491.0038
www.SomersetRidge.com

Underhill Farm Deer and Elk
187 21st Avenue
Moundridge KS, 67107
888.361.3261
www.UnderhillFarms.com

Restaurants and Markets—Kansas

Community Mercantile Coop
901 Iowa St.
Lawrence, KS 66044
www.CommunityMercantile.com

Local Burger
714 Vermont
Lawrence, KS 66044
785.856.7827
www.LocalBurger.com

WheatFields Bakery
904 Vermont Street
Lawrence, KS 66044
785.841.5553
www.WheatfieldsBakery.com

Michigan

Christopher B. Bedford
Strategic Consultant + Grassroots Organizer
"Healthy. Humane. Homegrown food systems."
6543 Hancock Road
Montague, MI 49437
231.893.3937
231.670.4817
chrisbedford@charter.net

Growing Hope
Amanda Edmonds
PO Box 980129
Ypsilanti, MI 48198
734.330.7576
www.GrowingHope.net

Halpin Family Farms
Fred Swaffer Jr
7897 Joy Rd
Kaleva, MI 49645
231.362.2450
www.HalpinFamilyFarms.com

Leopold Bros. Brewery
Todd and Scott Leopold
523 S Main St
Ann Arbor, MI 48104-2920
734.747.9806
www.LeopoldBros.com

Tabor Hill Winery and Restaurant
Restaurant and Winery of Slow Food Michiana
Director Paul Landeck
185 Mt. Tabor Road
Buchanan MI 49107
800.283.3363
www.TaborHill.com

Steve-n-Sons Sustenance
Raw Milk Cheese
14238 60th Avenue
Coopersville, MI 49404
616.997.1306

Zingerman's Bakehouse
Rachelle Baranger
3711 Plaza Drive
Ann Arbor, MI 48108
734.751.7255
www.ZingermansBakehouse.com

Zingerman's Creamery
Ann Lofgren and John Loomis
3723 Plaza Drive
Ann Arbor, MI 48108
734.929.0500
www.Zingermans.com

Zingerman's Coffee Company
Adrienne Voelker
620 Phoenix Drive
Ann Arbor, MI 48108
734.945.4711
www.Zingermans.com

Restaurants and Markets—Michigan

Ann Arbor Farmer's Market - Kerrytown District
Jessica Black, Market Manager
315 Detroit Street
Ann Arbor, MI 48104
734.994.3276
www.Ci.Ann-Arbor.mi.us/CommunityServices/Parks/
Farmers%20Market/Farmers_main.html

Arbor Farms
2103 W. Stadium
Ann Arbor, MI 48103
734.996.8111
www.ArborFarms.com

Eve
415 North 5th Ave.
Ann Arbor MI 48104
734.657.5770
www.EveTheRestaurant.com

The French Laundry
125 W. Shiawassee
Fenton. MI 48430
810.629.8852
www.LunchAndBeyond.com

Rattlesnake Club
300 River Place,
Detroit, MI 48207
313.567.4400
www.RattlesnakeClub.com

Sweetwater Local Foods Market
6543 Hancock Road
Montague, MI 49437
231.893.3937
231.670.4817
www.SweetwaterLocalFoodsMarket.org

Zingerman's Delicatessen
Grace Singleton
422 Detroit Street
Ann Arbor, MI 48104
734.663.3354
www.Zingermans.com

Zingerman's Roadhouse
Alex Young
2501 Jackson Road
Ann Arbor, MI 48103
734.663.3663
www.ZingermansRoadhouse.com

Minnesota

Andrej's European Pastries
Jan Gadzo
Chisholm, MN 55719
218.254.2520
www.PoticaWalnut.com

Rock Spring Farm
Chris and Kim Blanchard, family, and friends
3765 Highlandville Rd.
Spring Grove, MN 55974
563.735.5613
www.RSFarm.com

Shepherd's Way Sheep's Milk Cheese
Stephen and Jodi Read
8626 160th St. E.
Nerstrand, MN 55053
www.ShepherdsWayFarms.com

Schlangen Organic Farm
Alvin Schlangen
33236 Oakland Rd
Freeport, MN 56331
320.837.5347
www.MnOrganiceggs.com

White Earth Land Recovery Project
Winona LaDuke, Founding Director
607 Main Ave.
Callaway, MN 56521
218.375.2600
www.NativeHarvest.com

Restaurants and Markets—Minnesota

The Angry Trout Café (open May-Oct)
Chef George Wilkes
P.O. Box 973
Grand Marais, MN 55604
218.387.1265
www.AngryTroutCafe.com

Café Barbette
Chef Ty Hatfield
1600 W. Lake St.
Minneapolis, MN
612.827.5710
www.Barbette.com

Coco's to Geaux
Catering Business of Slow Food Lake Superior
Director Arlene Coco Buscombe
324 West Superior
Medical Arts Building
Duluth, MN 55802
218.740.3039

Heartland
Chef Lenny Russo
1806 St. Clair Avenue
St. Paul, MN 55105
651.699.3536
www.HeartlandRestaurant.com

Lucia's Restaurant and Wine Bar
Chef Lucia Watson
1432 West 31st St (at Hennepin)
Minneapolis, MN 55408-2605
612.825.1572
www.Lucias.com

St. Paul Farmers' Market
Locations throughout the city
May - October
www.StPaulFarmersMarket.com

Surdyk's
Wine, Liquor, Cheese
303 East Hennepin Avenue
Minneapolis, MN 55414
612-379-3232
www.Surdyks.com

Missouri

Fair Share Farm
Tom Ruggieri and Rebecca Graff
18613 Downing Road
Kearney, MO 64060
816.320.3763
www.FairShareFarm.com

Goatsbeard Farm
Artisanal Goat Cheeses
Ken and Jennifer Muno
11351 Callahan Creek Road
Harrisburg, MO 65256
573.875.0706
www.GoatsbeardFarm.com

Greystone Farms
Tim and Julie Walker
901 County Road 425
Fayette, MO 65248
660.248.3949

Kansas City Food Circle
A Project of Heart of America Action Linkage
PO Box 45195
Kansas City, MO 64171
816.374.5899
www.KcFoodCircle.org

Ozark Forest Mushrooms
Timber farms, "The Sinks"
HC 62 Box 460
Salem, MO 65560
314.531.9935
www.OzarkForest.com

Pierpont Farms
Rob and Angela Hemwall
8810 South Route N
Columbia, MO 65203
573.499.9851
www.PierpontFarms.com

Schlafly Taproom and Brewery
Stephen Hale, Brewmaster
2100 Locust St (@21st)
St. Louis, MO 63103
314.241.2337
www.Schlafly.com

Uprise Bakery
816A East Broadway
Columbia, MO 65201
573.256.2265

Restaurants and Markets—Missouri

Clayton Farmers' Market
Julie Ridlon
North Central and Maryland Ave
Clayton, MO
314.645.5807

Columbia Farmer's Market
1701 W. Ash
P.O. Box 10012
Columbia, MO 65205
573.449.GROW
www.ColumbiaFarmersMarket.org

Jasper's
(Restaurant of the Director of Slow Food KC)
Chef Jasper Mirabile
1201 W 103rd St
Kansas City, MO 64114
816.941.6600
www.JaspersKC.com

1924 Main
1924 Main St
Kansas City, MO 64108
816.472.1924
www.KansasCityMenus.com/1924main

Riddle's Penultimate Café and Wine Bar
6307 Delmar Blvd.
University City (St. Louis) Missouri 63130
314.725.6985
www.RiddlesCafe.com

The Root Cellar
814 E. Broadway
Columbia, MO 65201
573.443.5055

Savor
Chef Kirk Warner
4356 Lindell Blvd.
St. Louis, MO 63108
314.531.0220
www.SauceMagazine.com/Savor/

The Schlafly Bottleworks
7260 Southwest Avenue (at Manchester)
Maplewood, MO 63143
314.241.2337
www.Schlafly.com

The Smoke House Market
Thom Sehnert
16806 Chesterfield Airport Rd
Chesterfield, MO 63005
636.532.3314
www.SmokeHouseMarket.com

Ted Drewes Frozen Custard
6726 Chippewa St (Old Route 66)
St. Louis, MO 63109
314.481.2652
www.TedDrewes.com

The Wine Cellar and Bistro
505 Cherry Street
Columbia, MO 65201
573.442.7281
www.WineCellarBistro.com

Nebraska

Bluff Valley Farm Lamb
Ken and Mary Grace Thiltgers
Rulo, NE 68431
402.245.5460

Branched Oak Farm Cheeses
Doug and Krista Dittman
17015 NW 70th St
Raymond, NE 68428
402.783.2124

Common Good Farm
Ruth Chantry and Everett Lunquist
Raymond, NE 68428
402.783.9005
www.CommonGoodFarm.com

The Lithuanian Bakery
5217 South 33rd Avenue
Omaha, NE 68107
800.798.5217
www.LithuanianBakery.com

Nebraska Sustainable Agriculture Society
and Community (CROPS)
Executive Director's office:
Paul Rohrbaugh, RR 1 Box 66,
Steinhauer, NE 68441
402.869.2396
CROPS—Hartington Office
    Jill Wubben, PO Box 736,
    Hartington, NE 68739
    402.254.2289
www.NebSusAg.org

North Star Neighbors Lamb
Jim Knopik
Belgrade, NE 68623
308.536.2023

Pawnee Pride Pastured Beef and Turkey
Paul and Cyndie Rohrbaugh
Steinhauer, NE 68441
402.869.2396
www.PawneePride.com

SARE
North Central Region
University of Nebraska-Lincoln
13A Activities Bldg.
1734 N. 34th St.
Lincoln, NE 68583
402.472.7081
www.sare.org/ncrsare

Shadow Brook Farm Vegetables
Kevin and Charuth Loth
Lincoln, NE 68583
402.420.2283
www.ShadowBrk.com

Nebraska Food Cooperative
www.NebraskaFood.org

Restaurants and Markets—Nebraska

Maggie's Vegetarian Vittles
311 North 8th St
Lincoln, NE 68508
402.477.3959
www.MaggiesVegetarian.com

The Lithuanian Bakery and Café
7427 Pacific Street
Omaha, NE 68114
402.391.3503
www.LithuanianBakery.com

North Dakota

Northern Plains Sustainable Agriculture Society
Theresa Podoll, Executive Director
9824 79th St SE
Fullerton, ND 58441-9725
701.883.4304
www.npsas.org

Organic Crop Improvement Association
North Dakota Chapter #1
Darlene Kerzmann
HC2, Box 88
Garrison, ND 58540
701.743.4370
    North Dakota Chapter #2
    Richard Zundel, R.R. 1, Box 113
    Egely, ND 58433
    701.685.2423
www.ocia.org

The North Outback
Janet and Terry Jacobson
9173 95th St. NE
Wales, ND 58281
701-283-5195

Prairie Road Organic Farm
David, Dan and Theresa Podoll
9824 79th ST SE
Fullerton, ND 58441-9725

Sjorli Farms
Randy Rowse
10775 96th St NW
Noonan, ND 58765
701-925-5811

Restaurants and Markets—North Dakota

Hotel Donaldson & Restaurant HoDo
Chef Eric Inscho
101 Broadway
Fargo, ND 58102
701.478.1000 or 888.478.8768
www.HotelDonaldson.com

Ohio

Bluescreek Farm
Hormone/Antibiotic-Free Belgian Blue Beef
Cheryl and David Smith
14141 Hillview Rd
Marysville, OH 43040
513.644.2583
www.BluesCreekFarmMeats.com

Flying J Farm
Richard Jensen
5329 Van Fossen Road
Johnstown, OH 43031
www.FlyingJFarm.com

Local Matters Foodshed
Noreen Warnock
128 Clinton Heights
Columbus, OH 43202
614.447.2868

Harpersfield Winery
Patty and Adolph Ribic
6837 State Route 307
Geneva, OH 44041
440.466.4739
www.Harpersfield.com

Jeni's Ice Cream
In the Historic North Market
59 Spruce Sreet
Columbus, OH 43215
614.228.9960
www.JenisIceCreams.com

Just This Farm
Kevin Eigel
7657 Feder Rd.
Galloway, OH
614.853.1036
www.JustThisFarm.com

Lucy's Sweet Surrender
Michael Feigenbaum
12516 Buckeye Rd.
Cleveland, OH 44120
216.752.0828
www.LucysSweetSurrender.com

Northeast Ohio Foodshed Alliance
Brad Masi, c/o EDIC,
MPO Box 357, Oberlin, OH 44074
440.774.2906 or 216.225.6311

Ohio Ecological Food and Farm Association
PO Box 82234
Columbus OH 43202
614.421.2022
www.oeffa.org

Petticoat Jams
Madeleine Brodhead
2825 Euclid Heights Blvd. #4
Cleveland Heights, OH 44118
216.371.0412

Small Farm Research And Education Center
Silver Creek Farm
Ted and Molly Bartlett
6388-6399 Allyn Rd
Hiram, OH 44234
www.Sfrec-Scf.org

Pleasantview Farm
Perry Clutts
20361 Florence Chapel Pike
Circleville, OH 43113
740.474.2840
www.Pleasantiew-Farm.com

Speckled Hen Farm
Brooke Hayes-Lyman
5675 County Road 23
Cardington, OH 43315
419.768.2279
www.SpeckledHenFarm.com

Toad Hill Organic Farm
Tim and Jane Patrick
16261 Sapps Run Rd
Danville, OH 43014
740.599.9809
www.member.tripod.com/toadhill

Restaurants and Markets—Ohio

The Baricelli Inn
Chef/Owner Paul Minnillo
2203 Cornell Rd
Cleveland, OH 44106
216.791.6500
www.Baricelli.com

Clintonville Farmer's Market
Lynne Genter
4219North High St
Columbus, OH 43214
614.262.0226
www.ClintonvilleFarmersMarket.org

Coit Road Farmers' Market
Kathleen O'Neill Webb
15000 Woodworth Rd
East Cleveland, OH 44112
216.732.8518

Dragonfly
Organic, Neo-Vegan Cuisine
Magdiale Wolmark and Cristin Austin
247 King Ave
Columbus, OH 43201
614.298.9986
www.DragonflyNeoV.com

Fahrenheit
Chef Rocco Whalen
2417 Professor St.
Tremont, OH 44113
216.781.8858
www.FahrenheitTremont.com

North Market
Historic Public Market, Established in 1876
59 Spruce St
Columbus, OH 43215
614.463.9664
www.NorthMarket.com

The Refectory
Chef Richard Blondin
1092 Bethel Rd
Columbus, OH 43220
614.451.9774
www.TheRefectoryRestaurant.com

Oklahoma

Honey Hill Farm
Jo Ann and Jerry Logan
2501 Cedar Oak Dr
Edmond, OK 73013
405.341.5499

Keetonville Farms
Pastured Galloways
Marian and Dennis Bires
6555 E. 480 Rd.
Claremore, OK 74019
918.341.3908
dennisbires@lycos.com

Kokoa Chocolatier
Steven Howard
3410 S. Peoria Ave, Ste 200
Tulsa, OK 74105
918.742.4069
www.KokoaChocolatier.com

Oklahoma Food Cooperative
Robert Waldrop
1524 NW 21st St
Oklahoma City, OK 73106-4024
405.613.4688
www.OklahomaFood.coop

Three Springs Farm
Emily Oakley and Michael Appel
1367 Hwy 824
Oaks, OK 74368
918.868.5450
www.ThreeSpringsFarm.com

Restaurants and Markets—Oklahoma

The Cherry Street Farmers' Market
Lisa Merrel
The Tulsa Garden Center
918.852.2968
www.TheCherryStreetFarmersMarket.com

The Coach House
Chef Kurt Fleischfresser
6437 Avondale Dr
Nichols Hills, OK 73116
405.842.1000
www.Restaurant-Row.org/Coach

The Metro Wine Bar and Bistro
Chef Chad Willis
6418 N Western
Oklahoma City, OK 73116
405.840.9463
www.Restaurant-Row.org/Metro

The Museum Café
Chef Robert Black
Oklahoma City Museum of Art
415 Coach Dr
Oklahoma City, OK 73102
405.235.6262
www.OkcMoa.com/cafe

Table Ten
Chef Richard Clark
35 12 S. Peoria Ave
Tulsa, OK 74105
918.749-3310
www.Restauranteur.com/Tableten/

Vintage 1740
1740 S. Boston Avenue
Tulsa, OK 74119
918.582.0700
www.Vintage1740.com

South Dakota

Dakota Rural Action
P.O. Box 549
Brookings, SD 57006-0549
605.697.5204
drural@brookings.net
www.DakotaRural.org

Glacial Till Farm
Holly Whitesides and Jacob Limmer
44689 195th St.
Lake Norden, SD 57248
605.785.3173
www.GlacialTillfarm.com

InterTribal Bison Cooperative
2947 W Chicago St.
Rapid City, SD 57702
605.394.9730
www.ItbcBison.org

New Hope Farm & Prairie Granola
Zita Kwartek
5155 Lamb Rd.
Rapid City, SD 57703
605.393.2481

Restaurants and Markets—South Dakota

Breadroot Cooperative
130 Main St.
Rapid City, SD 57701
605-348-3331
www.BreadRoot.com

The Corn Exchange
Chef MJ Adams
727 Main St.
Rapid City, SD 57701
605.343.5070
www.CornExchange.com

Wisconsin

Blue Skies Berry Farm
Paul and Louise Maki
10320 N. Crocker Road
Brooklyn, WI 53521
608.455.2803
www.BlueSkiesForLamb.com

Blue Valley Gardens
Matthew and Susan Smith
2954 North Road
Blue Mounds, WI. 53517
www.mhtc.net/~blueval/

Elderberry Acres CSA and Market Farm
Renae Mitchell
7916 N. County Line Rd
Whitewater, WI 53190
262.473.2956

Future Fruit Farm
Bob, Ellen and Selena Lane
5363 Knobs Rd.
Ridgeway, WI 53582
608.924.1012

Home Grown Wisconsin
Suzanne Rubinstein
313 W. Beltline Highway, Suite 37
Madison, WI 53715
608.341.8939
www.HomeGrownWisconsin.com

Lathrop Farms
David and Jacqueline Lathrop
433 Jordan Drive
Mc Farland, WI 53558
608.835.7687
www.LathropFarms.com

Linda Halley
S. 3442 Wire Hollow Road
Viroqua, WI 54665
608.483.2143

Lovetree Farmstead Cheese
12413 Country Road Z
Grantsburg, WI 54840
715.488.2966
www.LovetreeFarmstead.com

Jordandal Farms
Eric and Carrie Johnson
W7977 Sunset Road
Argyle, WI 53504
608.328.1052
www.JordandalFarm.com

Michael Fields Agricultural Institute
W2493 County Road ES
East Troy, WI 53120
262.642.3303
www.MichaelFieldsAgInst.org

Midwest Organic and Sustainable Education Service
(MOSES)
Faye Jones, Executive Director
P.O. Box 339
Spring Valley, WI 54767
715.772.6819
www.MosesOrganic.org

Northwood Farms
James and Rebecca Goodman
E103 County Highway Q
Wonewoc, WI 535968
608.489.2291

River Chocolate Company
Allen Whitney
N 6461 Cty Rd N.
Beldenville, WI 54003
715.273.3731

Snug Haven Farm
Judy Hageman
1170 Hageman Dr.
Belleville, WI 53508
608.424.3296

Trautman Farms
Scott and Julie Trautman
2049 Skaalen Road
Stoughton, WI 53589
608.205.9798

Uplands Cheese Company, Inc.
Michael Gingrich
4540 County Rd. ZZ
Dodgeville, WI 53533
866.588.3443
www.UplandsCheese.com

Willow Creek Farm
Tony and Sue Renger
E5293 Ohio Road
Loganville, WI 53943
608.727.2224
www.WillowCreekPork.com

Restaurants and Markets—Wisconsin

The Back Porch Bistro
283 Victorian Village Drive
Elkhart Lake, WI 53020
920.876.3645
www.Vicvill.com

Chez Marché
Bonni Miller
108 S. Main St.
Waupaca, WI 54981
715.256.2672
www.ChezMarcheCafe.blogspot.com

L'Etoile
Chef/Owner Tory Miller
25 North Pinckney Street
Madison, WI 53703
608.251.0500
www.Letoile-Restaurant.com

Gilbert's
Chef Ken Hnilo
327 Wrigley Drive
Lake Geneva, WI 53147
262.248.6680
www.GilbertsRestaurant.com

Harvest
Chef Jeff Orr
21 N. Pinckney St.
Madison, WI 53703
608.255.6075
www.Harvest-Restaurant.com

Lombardino's
Marcia and Patrick O'Halloran
2500 University Avenue
Madison, Wisconsin 53705
608.238.1922
www.Lombardinos.com

Marigold Kitchen
Phillip Hurley and John Gadau
118 S. Pinckney
Madison, WI 53703
608.661.5559
www.MarigoldKitchen.com

Riverview Terrace Café
Chris Staples
5607 County Hwy C
Spring Green, WI 53588
608.588.7937

The Dane County Farmers' Market
Capitol Square, Madison, WI 53703
866.424.6714
www.MadFarmMkt.org

The Washington Hotel, Restaurant & Culinary School
354 Rangeline Road
Washington Island, WI 54246
920.847.2169
www.TheWashingtonHotel.com

Additional Slow Food Resources

Slow Food U.S.A. National Office
20 Jay St, Suite 313
Brooklyn, NY 11201
718.260.8000
www.SlowFoodUSA.org

Slow Food International Office
Via Mendicità Istruita, 8
12042 Bra (CN) - Italy
Tel 39.0172.419.611
www.SlowFood.com
international@slowfood.com

Slow Food Foundation for Biodiversity
Via della Mendicità Istruita, 14
12042 Bra (Cn) – Italy
39.0172.419.701
foundation@SlowFood.com
www.SlowFoodFoundation.org

The University of Gastronomic Sciences
www.unisg.it/eng/index.htm

Terra Madre
Via della Mendicità Istruita, 14
12042 Bra (CN)
Italy 39.0172.472911
www.terramadre2008.org

Recommended Reading

Over the last few years, members of Slow Food USA's online forum have built a reading list for those who wish to understand the Slow Food philosophy. Despite the fact that I have added a few more to the list, it is by no means complete. As internet technology and trends continue to evolve, the forum has been replaced by a blog—www.slowfoodblog.org—but I've preserved the list by adding it here.

Many of these books were indispensable during the research for this book, and still more were overpowering influences on my career. If you are serious about food, you may wish to add all these books to your shelf.—kmf

Against the Grain: How Agriculture has Hijacked Civilization by Richard Manning. New York : North Point Press, 2004.

The Botany of Desire: A Plant's Eye View of the World by Michael Pollan. New York : Random House, 2001.

Bread Alone: Bold Fresh Loaves from Your Own Hands by Daniel Leader: New York : W. Morrow, 1993

Cheese Primer by Steve Jenkins. Workman Publishing, 1996

The Glorious Foods of Greece: Traditional Recipes from the Islands, Cities, and Villages by Diane Kochilas New York : Workman Pub., 1996.

Chez Panisse Vegetables; Chez Panisse Café Cookbook; Chez Panisse Fruit; Chez Panisse Menu Cookbook; Chez Panisse Cooking; Fanny at Chez Panisse; Chez Panisse Pasta, Pizza, Calzone all by the inimitable Alice Waters, All published in New York by HarperCollins, various years.

Cider, Hard and Sweet by Ben Watson. Woodstock, VT, Countryman Press, 2000

Cod: A Biography of the Fish That Changed the World by Mark Kurlansky New York, Walker and Co., 1997.

Coming Home to Eat: The Pleasures and Politics of Local Food by Gary Paul Nabhan. New York : Norton, 2002.

Cooking by Hand by Paul Bertolli New York, Clarkson Potter, 2003

The Debt to Pleasure by John Lanchester. New York, Henry Holt and Co., 1996

Diet For a New America by John Robbins, Walpole, NH : Stillpoint, 1987.

Eat Here: Reclaiming Homegrown Pleasures in a Global Supermarket by Brian Halweil. New York : W.W. Norton, 2004.

Epicurean Delights: The Life and Times of James Beard by Evan Jones, New York, Alfred A Knopf, 1990

Epitaph for a Peach by David Mas Masumoto. San Francisco, HarperSanFrancisco, 1996

Fast Food Nation: The Dark Side of the All-American Meal by Eric Schlosser, Boston : Houghton Mifflin, 2001

Fatal Harvest: the Tragedy of Industrial Agriculture, edited by Andrew Kimbrell Washington, D.C. : Island Press, 2002.

Food Fight: The Inside Story of the Food Industry, America's Obesity Crisis, and What We Can Do About It by Kelly D. Brownell, Chicago : Contemporary Books, 2004.

Food Politics: How the Food Industry Influences Nutrition and Health by Marion Nestle. Berkeley : University of California Press, 2002.

Four Seasons in Five Senses: Things Worth Savoring by David Mas Masumoto. New York : WW Norton, 2003

A gracious plenty : recipes and recollections from the American South / John T. Edge for the Center for the Study of Southern Culture at the University of Mississippi. by John T Edge and Ellen Rolfes. New York : Putnam, 1999

Grassland: The History, Biology, Politics and Promise of the American Prairie by Richard Manning. New York, Viking, 1995.

Harvest Son: Planting Roots in American Soil by David Mas Masumoto. New York ; London : W. W. Norton and Co., 1998.

Holy Cows and Hog Heaven: The Food Buyer's Guide to Farm Friendly Food by Joel Salatin, Polyface, 2005

Honey from a Weed : Fasting and Feasting in Tuscany, Catalonia, the Cyclades and Apulia by Patience Gray, New York : Lyons and Burford Publishers, 1996

Hungering For America: Italian, Irish and Jewish Foodways in the Age of Migration by Hasia Diner, Cambridge, Mass. ; London : Harvard University Press, 2001

In Defense of Food: An Eater's Manifesto by Michael Pollan, New York : Penguin Press, 2008

In Praise of Slowness: How a Worldwide Movement is Challenging the Cult of Speed by Carl Honoré, San Francisco, HarperSanFrancisco, 2004

Italian Cheese edited by Piero Sardo, Gigi Piumatti, and Roberto Rubino, Slow Food Arcigola Editore, Bra, Italy 1999-2000

Italian Food Artisans by Pamela Sheldon Johns, San Francisco : Chronicle Books, 2000.

Last Chance to Eat: The fate of taste in a Fast Food World by Gina Mallet New York : W. W. Norton, 2004

The Last Days of Haute Cuisine by Patrick Kuh New York, Penguin Books, 2001

Local Flavors: Cooking and Eating From America's Farmers' Markets by Deborah Madison, New York : Broadway Books, 2002.

Le Monde n'est pas une marchandise : Entretiens avec Gilles Luneau by Jose Bove and François Dufour, Paris, Pocket, 2004

Mountain Spirits: A Chronicle of Corn Whiskey from King James' Ulster Plantation to America's Appalachians and the Moonshine Life by Joe Dabney New York : Charles Scribner's Sons, 1974

Much depends on dinner : the Extraordinary History and Mythology, Allure and Obsessions, Perils and Taboos of an Ordinary Meal by Margaret Visser, Grove Press, 1999

My Vegetable Love: A Journal of a Growing Season by Carl H. Klaus Iowa City : University of Iowa Press, 1996

Near a Thousand Tables: A History of Food by Felipe Fernandez-Armesto New York ; London : Free Press, 2002

No Foreign Food: The American Diet in Time and Place by Richard Pillsbury Boulder, Colo. : Westview Press, 1998.

Noodling for Flatheads by Burkhard Bilger New York : Scribner, 2000

Nourishing Traditions by Sally Fallon, Washington, DC : NewTrends Pub., 2001.

Olives: Life and Lore of a Noble Fruit by Mort Rosenblum, New York : North Point Press, 1996

The Omnivore's Dilemma: A Natural History of Four Meals by Michael Pollan, Penguin Press, 2006

The Physiology of Taste: Or Meditations on Transcendental Gastronomy by Jean Anthelme Brillat-Savarin, Washington, DC : Counterpoint, 1995

The Pleasures of Slow Food by Corby Kummer, San Francisco : Chronicle Books, 2002

The Real Food Revival: Aisle By Aisle, Morsel By Morsel by Sherri Brooks Vinton and Ann Clark Espuelas, New York : Jeremy P. Tarcher/Penguin, 2005

Renewing America's Food Traditions: Saving and Savoring the Continent's Most Endangered Foods Edited by Gary Paul Nabhan with foreword by Deborah Madison, Chelsea Green Publishing, 2008

Savoring the Seasons of the Northern Heartland by Lucia Watson and Beth Dooley, New York : Knopf : Distributed by Random House, 1994

Serious Pig: An American in Search of His Roots by John Thorne with Matt Lewis Thorne, New York, North Point Press, 1996

Slow Food: The Case for Taste by Carlo Petrini, et al. New York : Columbia University Press, 2003

Slow Food: Collected Thoughts on Taste, Tradition, and the Honest Pleasures of Food by Carlo Petrini (Editor), et al White River Junction, Vt. : Chelsea Green Pub., 2001

The Slow Food Companion by Sarah Weiner, Bra, Italy, Slow Food Editore, 2005

The Slow Food Guide to Chicago Restaurants, Markets, Bars by Portia Belloc-Lowndes and Kelly Gibson, White River Junction, VT, Chelsea Green, 2004

The Slow Food Guide to New York City Restaurants, Markets, Bars by Patrick Martins and Ben Watson, White River Junction, VT, Chelsea Green, 2003

The Slow Food Guide to San Francisco Restaurants, Markets, Bars by Eleanor Bertino, Sylvan Brackett, Wendy Downing and Sue Moore, White River Junction, VT, Chelsea Green, 2006

Slow Food Nation: Why Our Food Should Be Good, Clean, And Fair, by Carlo Petrini with a foreword by Alice Waters, New York : Rizzoli, 2007

Smokestack Lightning by Lois Eric Elie, New York : Farrar, Straus and Giroux, 1996

Southern Food: At Home, on the Road, in History by John Egerton, Chapel Hill : University of North Carolina Press, 1993

The Splendid Table Recipes from Emilia-Romagna, the heartland of northern Italian food by Lynn Rossetto Kasper, New York : W. Morrow, 1992

The Unsettling of America: Culture and Agriculture by Wendell Berry, San Francisco : Sierra Club Books, 1996

A Very Small Farm by William Paul Winchester, Tulsa, Okl : Council Oak Books, 1996

Why Some Like it Hot by Gary Paul Nabhan Washington, DC Island Press/Shearwater Books, 2004

A World of Presidia: Food, Culture and Community, Bra, Italy, Slow Food Editore, 2004

Zingerman's Guide to Good Eating by Ari Weinzweg, Boston : Houghton Mifflin, 2003

… And absolutely everything MFK Fisher ever wrote.

About Slow Food

You are encouraged to join the movement! Slow Food maintains all people's right to taste - and gains its momentum through its members' hands-on dedication to change. We currently have over 80,000 members, in 100 countries, spreading the word and changing the world! Your participation and your voice make our message stronger.

As a member, there are many ways to get involved and be heard. Your local Slow Food group (Convivia) is the first point of contact - joining you to a larger international movement of people dedicated to protecting taste, culture and the environment as universal social values. You will have an opportunity to participate in all our programs and attend all local, national and international events. Here is a sampling of member benefits:

¶A personal membership card

¶The *Slow Food Companion*

¶Four issues of the newsletter, the *Snail*

¶The Annual *Slow Food Almanac*

¶The right to attend all events organized by the Slow Food movement around the world

¶Discounts on all Slow Food publications and merchandise.

When you donate to Slow Food, your funds directly contribute to our movement to create a food system that is "good, clean and fair." Your helping hand makes an enormous difference, as we reach across cultures, continents and out to new people to educate the world about the Slow Life. You are making the following programs possible:

¶Ark USA

¶Slow Food in Schools

¶Terra Madre

¶The *Snail* Newsletter

¶The Slow Food Foundation for Biodiversity

¶The University of Gastromic Science

Slow Food U.S.A. is a non-profit organization. An individual membership is $60.00 per year and a couple's membership is $75.00 per year. A new low-cost membership level is due to be introduced at Slow Food Nation in San Francisco Labor Day, 2008. Your membership dues are tax deductible, except for the $15 allocated for publications.

For information on membership, donations or starting a new convivium, please contact Slow Food U.S.A.'s National Office at 718.260.8000

Local Slow Food Convivia in the Heartland.

These are the Convivia that Slow Food USA has established throughout the Heartland as of press time. This list is growing far faster than the name would suggest. To get up to the moment information on these groups be sure to check the Slow Food USA website (www.SlowFoodUSA.org).

Don't see a convivium near you? Contact the national office through the above website and they'll get you started building one! It's not difficult, and it is a lot of fun.

ILLINOIS
Slow Food Chicago
Slow Food Goose Creek
Slow Food Springfield

INDIANA
Slow Food Bloomington
Slow Food Indianapolis

IOWA
Slow Food Ames
Slow Food Clear Lake
Slow Food Des Moines
Slow Food Iowa City
Slow Food Pella

MICHIGAN
Slow Food Detroit
Slow Food Grand Traverse
Slow Food Huron Valley (Ann Arbor)
Slow Food Michiana (Buchanan)
Slow Food Red Cedar (Lansing)
Slow Food West Michigan Potawatomi
    (Grand Rapids)

MINNESOTA
Slow Food Carleton College
Slow Food Lake Superior (Duluth)
Slow Food Minnesota (Minneapolis)
Slow Food Rochester

MISSOURI
Slow Food Kansas City
Slow Food Katy Trail (Columbia)
Slow Food St. Louis

NEBRASKA
Slow Food Nebraska (Lincoln/Omaha)

OHIO
Slow Food Columbus
Slow Food Maumee Valley (Toledo)
Slow Food Northern Ohio Cleveland
Slow Food Ohio River Valley

OKLAHOMA
Slow Food Oklahoma City
Slow Food Tulsa

WISCONSIN
Slow Food Chippewa
Slow Food Madison
Slow Food University of Wisconsin – Madison
Slow Food Wisconsin SE Milwaukee

Index

Symbols

The Ice Cube Press began publishing in 1993 to focus on the natural world and to better understand how people can best live together in the communities they inhabit. Since this time, we've been recognized by a number of well-known writers, including Gary Snyder, Gene Logsdon, Wes Jackson, Patricia Hampl, Jim Harrison, Annie Dillard, Kathleen Norris and Barry Lopez. We've published a number of well-known authors as well, including Mary Swander, Jim Heynen, Mary Pipher, Bill Holm, Carol Bly, Marvin Bell, Debra Marquart, Ted Kooser, Stephanie Mills, Bill McKibben and Paul Gruchow. Check out our books at our web site, with booksellers, or in museum shops, then discover why we are dedicated to "hearing the other side."

Ice Cube Press
205 N Front Street
North Liberty, Iowa 52317-9302
steve@icecubepress.com
www.icecubepress.com

from high and low, near and far
thanks, hugs, kisses and cheers to
Fenna Marie & Laura Lee
official contributors on the road to bliss